CHINESE
BUSINESS
ETIQUETTE

WITHDRAWN
From Toronto Public Library

CHINESE BUSINESS ETIQUETTE

THE PRACTICAL POCKET GUIDE
REVISED AND UPDATED

Stefan H. Verstappen

Stone Bridge Press • *Berkeley, California*

Published by
Stone Bridge Press
P. O. Box 8208, Berkeley, CA 94707
TEL 510-524-8732
sbp@stonebridge.com • www.stonebridge.com

Printed in the United States of America.

2019 2018 2017 2016 2015   10 9 8 7 6 5 4 3 2 1

LIBRARY OF CONGRESS CATALOGING-IN-PUBLICATION DATA
Verstappen, Stefan H.
 Chinese business etiquette : the practical pocket guide, revised
and updated / Stefan H. Verstappen.—Revised and Updated
Edition.
    pages cm
 ISBN 978-1-61172-020-4 (paperback)
 ISBN 978-1-61172-912-2 (e-book)
1. Business etiquette—China. 2. Corporate culture—China. I.
Title.
 HF5389.3.C6V47 2015
 395.5'20951—dc23

                        2015009942

Contents

Preface

This pocket guide can act as a refresher and handy reference on common business and social protocols for anyone traveling and doing business in China, Taiwan, and Hong Kong, as well as a basic introduction on this subject for those responsible for greeting visitors from China.

The information provided herein will help you understand Chinese business culture better in order to make friends, negotiate deals, and improve your overall chances of a successful experience working with the Chinese.

No single book can sum up a country as diverse and complex as China.

Although by necessity providing a general overview of a culture involves some stereotyping, keep in mind that the Chinese are also individuals with a wide range of experiences and that they may or may not conform to the guidelines offered below.

In addition, China is rapidly changing, and while the foundations of etiquette and business practices will likely remain the same, new trends and innovations are constantly evolving and may not be covered in this book.

■■■ ABOUT THE 2ND EDITION

In the seven years since the first publication of this book, China's economy has exceeded even the optimistic forecasts made back then and has surpassed that of the U.S. to make China the largest economy and trading nation in the world.

Currently, China's middle class is booming. This growing segment makes up 25% of the population, has an income between $7,250 and $62,500 a year, and holds post-secondary degrees.

China's culture is likewise experiencing a rapid transformation, going from values and attitudes based on an Old World agrarian culture to those of a more efficient and more ruthless culture of entrepreneurship and fierce competition.

Over the years, although many areas have opened up for foreign investment, non-Chinese outsiders are not always able to do business on equal terms with Chinese entrepreneurs.

For example, foreigners need more capital to set

up a business in China, and their investments will be more closely scrutinized than those of Chinese firms. There are still numerous business opportunities available, but the Chinese are more confident and no longer so open to joint ventures, preferring to go it on their own.

Meanwhile, Taiwan is beginning to experience an economic slowdown as China's manufacturing capabilities increase. Taiwan's standard of living and average worker wages have always been much higher than on the mainland, but these enable China to undercut Taiwan with cheaper labor costs. While Taiwan is now subcontracting much of its manufacturing to countries with even lower wage, rates such as Vietnam, Bangladesh, and Indonesia, this will do nothing for the average Taiwanese worker and unemployment in Taiwan will grow.

Hong Kong is likewise starting to suffer as a result of China's economic growth. In the past, Hong Kong's claim to fame was that it was once a British colony and the only port with which to trade with the old Communist China. Before the Communist takeover, Hong Kong was just a seedy backwater port town. Since its return to Chinese control, albeit with special status, Hong Kong's previous monopoly on Chinese trade has been broken by the rising superstar business cities of Shanghai and Shenzhen. The notorious sweatshops of old Hong Kong have all but disappeared, and it makes little sense to ship manufactured goods from China through Hong Kong when they could be shipped direct.

And even though Hong Kong has transitioned away from manufacturing and into finance and banking, her old rival Shanghai has regained its title as the business capital of China. What will become of Hong Kong is uncertain—its exemption from gambling and prostitution prohibitions will no doubt increase the city's popularity as a tourist destination.

China is also following Singapore, Taiwan, and Hong Kong in its curiosity about and then desire for Western ideas and culture. A hundred years ago, China was fascinated by Western manufactured products yet shunned Western culture. Now, ironically, in China there is scarcely a manufactured product made in the West but instead a greater interest in Western culture. For example, there is Chinese hip hop, white instead of the traditional red wedding dresses are the rage, and English is the most popular second language.

With the importation of Western values and economic prosperity come increasing signs that the social ills of long ago—prostitution, street crime, gambling loan sharking, drugs—are returning. This issue was not included in the first edition of this book since the chance of any Westerner having to deal it was remote.

However, criminality now forms a much larger part of the current culture of China and thus is discussed in this new edition.

While many things in China are in a state of flux, Chinese business and social etiquette remains deeply rooted in millennia-old tradition and is not likely to change suddenly into a model of Western business culture. Chinese will continue do things the way they have done them in the past.

Introduction

*It is a doctrine of war not to assume the enemy
will not come, but rather to rely on one's readiness
to meet him; not to presume that he will not
attack, but rather to make one's self invincible.*

Sun Tzu, *The Art of War*

There is a story often told of how a British industri-
alist in the early 19th century speculated that if only
they could persuade every Chinese to add just one
inch of material to the length of their shirts, it would
keep British textile factories running for generations.
Since Roman times the lure of the China market has
drawn adventurers and entrepreneurs from all over
the world, but much like the California Gold Rush,
only a few made fortunes, while the vast majority lost.

Since the normalization of trade and China's
acceptance into the World Trade Organization in
2001, the lure of vast, untapped markets has drawn

companies from all over the world. Though China has huge market potential, thus far few foreign companies have found equally huge success.

Even the Japanese and Taiwanese have had difficulties exploiting China's markets despite having closer ties to and a better understanding of China. There are many reasons for this. China's experience under Communist rule from the 1950s on was dramatically different from, say, the experiences of Japan or Taiwan during the same era. The result is a unique cultural and business landscape, which is still very much a factor in today's China. The vast geographical and cultural differences of China are more akin to the European Union, with Chinese provinces being as different culturally as, say, Italy is to Finland. Adding to the confusion is the accumulation of 4,000 years worth of culture, all of which have created a dynamic business environment that is constantly evolving.

While there are numerous difficulties in doing business in China, the potential rewards are enormous. If you wish to do business in China, the most important step you can take toward establishing a successful and rewarding relationship with your Chinese partners is to familiarize yourself with the basic principles of Chinese business culture. Once in China, be prepared to enter into a long learning curve whose lessons can only be mastered in the trenches.

■■■ THE IMPORTANCE OF ETIQUETTE

The first rule of Chinese business culture is that business *is* personal. Your success will depend on how much your Chinese peers like and respect you. Unlike Western countries, where professionalism implies being emotionally removed from the business process, in China business people make decisions according to their personal feelings about the deal and about the personalities of those involved in the deal. First impressions are a key component in all Chinese business negotiations. By learning the basics of Chinese business etiquette, you will have already taken the first step in making a good first, and lasting, impression.

Be warned, it will be impossible to anticipate or avoid all of the problems of dealing with Chinese business people and bureaucrats. The differences in culture and language can turn a simple business procedure into a test of endurance. If there is a Golden Rule of dealing with the Chinese, it is this: never lose your cool. The unique pressures of doing business in a foreign country can easily lead to frustration, anger, impatience, and ultimately condescension. Such attitudes will not go unnoticed. Patience, professionalism, and perseverance are the qualities that will eventually lead you to success.

Initially, it may seem as though the Western executive is at a distinct disadvantage doing business in

China, but there is an upside: Western executives have unique advantages over their Chinese counterparts.

The first advantage is directness. Because so much in Chinese social and office interactions depends on the all-important concept of "face," many Chinese tend to be reluctant to make quick decisions and will look to find a consensus before committing to a decision. As a result, Chinese managers can be notoriously hesitant and indirect. But as a Westerner, you are outside the political circle and are not expected to play the game of office politics. Thus, you can be more direct in voicing opinions and ideas that others cannot for fear of upsetting coworkers. Rather than be offended, many Chinese will appreciate the Westerner's straightforward approach and ability to get to the point.

The second advantage Westerners enjoy is that the Chinese do not expect them to understand and comply with Chinese etiquette. Should you make some cultural *faux pas*, the Chinese staff will be forgiving and take it all in good humor. This gives you considerable leeway socially as well as in making deals, since you can be more aggressive during negotiations and feign ignorance if you stretch the limits of negotiations too far. Conversely, should you display some knowledge of Chinese etiquette and culture, you will almost immediately make a good impression and be considered an educated and culturally sophisticated person, an honor in a society that places the highest value on education. This will put you on the leading edge of the learning curve and enable you to make friends, conduct business successfully, and enjoy your experience.

Lastly, despite the occasional cultural misunderstandings and prejudices, most Chinese admire Westerners and Western civilization. Westerners are considered somewhat exotic, and there is a certain cachet in having Western friends and business partners. With tact and a subtle manner you can use your almost celebrity-like status to great advantage.

The advantages and disadvantages thus balanced, it is back to intelligence and personality to determine success.

Foundations of Chinese Culture

To be able under all circumstances to practice
five things constitutes perfect virtue; these five
things are gravity, generosity of soul, sincerity,
earnestness, and kindness.

Confucius, *The Analects*

A great source of national pride for the Chinese is their uninterrupted, almost 4,000-year-long cultural history, making China the world's oldest continuous civilization. Chinese history is vast, complicated, and mysterious, but for the Western executive, knowing a little about China's history will provide insights into what attitudes one can expect.

There are four historical traditions that underlie all of Chinese culture.

■■■ I. AGRARIANISM

The first tradition is agrarianism. China was one of the first civilizations to develop farming, and most Chinese then, as now, lived in rural farming communities. These communities, often separated from outside help by China's mountainous geography, were vulnerable to numerous natural disasters. In order to survive, people learned to band together, forming communal—rather than individualistic—societies. Thus, what is good for the village always trumps what is good for the individual, and cooperation and obedience to the group is favored over independent thinkers and mavericks. This agrarian mindset prevails today even among China's modern city dwellers.

Though ruthlessly exploited by the ruling class, farmers were the producers of China's wealth and held a higher status over merchants, who were thought to live parasitically off the labors of others. The prejudice that commerce and business are somewhat shady activities prevails, and not without good reason.

Another aspect of China's agrarian culture that greatly influences Chinese business attitudes is geography. Surrounded by rough terrain that in the past supported only pastoral economies, the sophisticated Chinese agrarian and urban culture looked down on pastoralists; since these "lesser" peoples constituted their only experience with foreigners, the Chinese came to assume all foreigners were culturally inferior.

From the time of its unification more than 2,000 years ago, China has viewed itself as the center of culture in the world; hence, the Chinese name for China is *Zhongguo,* or "Middle Kingdom."

In the past, few foreign manufactured goods could compare to those that were Chinese-made. China has long seen itself as an export nation: grudgingly importing raw materials, but seldom goods manufactured from outside. During the West's industrial revolution, China admitted some Western products were superior, and markets for these opened up briefly, but in recent years China has quickly closed the technology gap and may well be in the lead again. The old attitude of "There is nothing we lack" is again prevalent in international trade, with the result that buying Chinese products and services is relatively uncomplicated, while selling products or services to the Chinese can be as challenging as selling air conditioners to Eskimos.

■■■ II. PHILOSOPHIC TRADITIONS

What you do not want done to yourself, do not do to others.

Confucius, *The Analects*

Despite being revered as a deity and having temples dedicated to him, Confucius, contrary to general impressions, was not a religious figure. Confucius (6th to 5th century BCE) was a moralist and social engineer who taught that a successful political system was dependent on creating a properly ordered social hierarchy.

Confucius's writings have survived many an emperor's book-burning campaign because he viewed society as pyramid-shaped, with a paramount ruler, the emperor, conveniently at the apex. Loyalty and fealty trickled down through the chain of command that started with the emperor, then to the middle layers of officials and administrators, and finally to families at the bottom. As long as everyone behaved in accordance with his or her social position, then government and society would be harmonious, and everyone would be prosperous and happy.

The keystone of making this system hold together is that the emperor must be the ideal of gentlemanly virtue. While loyalty works from the bottom up, corruption works from the top down, epitomized by the Chinese saying *A fish starts rotting at the head*. Hence, the leader of any group must present himself as the embodiment of self-discipline and virtue.

In this Confucian system, the family functioned much like a feudal barony. The father represented the head of the family unit or clan, while brothers, sons, mothers, and daughters ranked in descending order of influence. Like a barony, the male head of the family was answerable to the next level of civil authority, and if anyone in his family clan caused an offense the male head and the entire family were held accountable.

Under Qin Shi Huangdi, China's first emperor (221–206 BCE), there was a form of capital punishment known as the punishment of clan extinction (*miezu*), in which all members of a family clan, comprising grandparents to great grandchildren, would be executed should even one member of the clan commit a capital offense. Naturally, with such consequences hanging over their heads, family members kept a close eye on each other to ensure that everyone kept their proper place.

The family unit was organized like the government model in microcosm, with each member having a clearly defined relationship to the other. Family members addressed each other by titles such as "Elder Daughter" or "Younger Brother" rather than by given name. Unlike most Western societies, the Chinese have evolved specific titles for designating familiar relationships, such as "Father's elder brother" (*bo fu*) and "Father's sister's husband" (*gu fu*), as well as for every possible family relationship. There would thus be eight different titles for relationships that we would simply call "Uncle."

Those who were without family were generally pitied, but also viewed with suspicion since without a family structure to keep them in line, they were thought to be more likely to commit insurrections or crimes.

The values of the Confucian system still form the basis for Chinese etiquette exemplified by the following protocols:

Respect Your Superiors

Deference to rank is strongly enforced. As in the pyramid structure, lower classes are expected to respect those above them. Listing from the top down, the classes were scholars, officials, farmers, artisans, and merchants. Scholars and officials made up the respected "gentry" while the lowest classes consisted of outcast groups, such as actors, prostitutes, boat people, and slaves. This deference to social authority applies both outside the family and within it.

Respect Your Elders

Within the family the same hierarchy is in place. The eldest male was usually head of the family and had to be obeyed by all. Superiority based on age applied to all members; younger brothers had to respect and obey elder brothers, as younger sisters did elder sisters. As in all paternal societies, females were expected to defer to males, although the chief wife of the head of the family had much power over running the household and often became a domestic tyrant, especially toward the daughters-in-law. The widespread Chinese respect for age and seniority deems an older person as more experienced, wiser, and thereby superior to those younger.

Family Values

Confucian tradition positioned the family as the basic societal unit and became one of the first advocates of strong family values. Each individual within the family was encouraged to be a "team player," first within the family team, then within the societal team. Confucius simply codified the existing agrarian strategy of collectivist cooperation and applied it to society as a whole. These values are ideally suited to family-run businesses, and indeed most private Chinese businesses are family owned and operated. It is in the Chinese family business that Confucian ethics are strongest. Typically, those businesses will have a dominant family head, long-range goals, and interfamily obligations, and will be financed and held accountable only within the family.

Lao Tzu (Lao Zi)

One who excels in employing others humbles himself before them. This is known as the virtue of non-contention.

Lao Tzu, *Dao De Jing*

Contemporaneous with Confucius was Lao Tzu, the reputed founder of Daoism and philosophical mirror of Confucius. While Confucius sought to understand the role of man and society, Lao Tzu sought to explain the fundamental principles of man and nature. From Daoism comes the concept of Yin (the feminine, dark, and passive force) and Yang (the masculine, light, and active force), and their dual relationship.

In Daoism, the universe is a mixture of these two forces that both oppose and complement one another simultaneously. There are no black-and-white issues but rather an infinite number of shades of gray. From Daoism comes the new-age platitude of "go with the flow," a strategy of compromising oneself with the existing forces at play to find the middle ground or "The Way." Some of the attitudes based on Daoism can be a great source of frustration for Western sensibilities. One example is the "don't worry about it until it breaks" approach, which has been known to drive Western-educated quality control, maintenance engineering, and troubleshooting personnel to drink. Another example is seen during contract negotiations: Western legal minds that seek to define all aspects of an agreement are frustrated by the Daoist principle of there being no truly right or wrong contracts but only contracts with various degrees of correctness. That is, the Chinese see all clauses as being open to further compromise even after the signatories have signed.

■■■ III. CHINESE WRITING

The third historical tradition is the Chinese way of writing. The Chinese written language is similar to Egyptian hieroglyphics in that it uses stylized pictographs to create words and combinations of pictures together to create more complex words. This allows all 200+–different-dialect-speaking peoples to be able to read the same language, since each written character conveys the same meaning. This system is opposite of phonetic transcription systems such as our Latin alphabet wherein the characters tell you how to speak the word but not the word's meaning. Written Chinese has been a major force in uniting the many diverse dialects and cultures that have always made up China's land and people.

To read a Chinese character requires you to see

the whole picture together, not just the component root elements (known as radicals). This has led to a mentality that sees the forest over the trees, one that chooses a big-picture approach over one concerned with the smaller details.

The Chinese written language has one major drawback: its complexity.

A Western child can learn all twenty-six letters of the alphabet in under a year. Chinese schoolchildren, however, are required to memorize thousands of complex characters, and this can take many years of study. It is estimated that one needs to know about 3,000 characters just to be able to read a newspaper. In addition, while roman letters require at most four strokes of the pen to write, Chinese characters may require multiple strokes to write one character. Thus the ability to memorize is emphasized at the expense of the ability to improvise.

The complexity of the Chinese writing system has caused education to be a longer and more intensive process. This has also helped mold the Chinese attitude toward time, their belief that nothing of importance can be accomplished quickly.

For example, using our Latin alphabet, with only twenty-six letters, everything can be filed alphabetically under only twenty-six categories. To look up a word in the dictionary we need only know how it sounds and can easily follow a logical flow chart from first letter to second letter, etc., to find the word we want. For Western minds, organizing things according to alphabetical categories is a natural inclination.

Conversely, the Chinese written language contains more than 47,000 characters with no reasonable way of organizing them into categories. Chinese scholars have devised dictionaries that attempt to organize words by either their stroke count (number of strokes required to write each word) or by radicals. Both methods are complex, there being up to 57 strokes or 214 radicals, and even then, these categories have many exceptions to the rule. To look up a word in a Chinese dictionary you would first need to know how it is written, which of course negates the need to look it up. If you did not know how to write the word you would then need to know either how many strokes were required to write it, or which of the 214 radicals the word employs. While looking up a word in an English dictionary can take as little as a few seconds, looking up a word in a Chinese dictionary can take a very long time.

Chinese categorization systems like this can thus employ a combination of 57 and 214 headings. This can cause some frustration for Westerners, who tend to think in terms of linear progression, like on a computer flow chart. Chinese, in contrast, tend to think in a holistic manner. What is a simple, clear-cut progression for Westerners is not viewed as such by the Chinese.

■■■ IV. HISTORICAL ATTITUDES TOWARD FOREIGNERS

The fourth historical tradition is the Chinese people's wariness of foreigners. China's interaction with foreigners has a long history of unpleasantness for the Chinese. Since earliest times, China suffered sporadic raids and invasions from the nomadic horsemen in the north starting with the Xiongnu, or Huns, in the 5th century BCE. In the 12th century, the Mongols invaded and established the Yuan dynasty and began an ethnic-cleansing campaign whose Han Chinese casualities are estimated at upward of 50 million.[1] Again, in the 16th century, another group of nomadic horsemen from the northeast, the Manchu, invaded and established the last Chinese dynasty known as the Qing dynasty. The Manchu regarded native or Han Chinese as akin to livestock and enforced the purposefully humiliating rule that men must braid their hair into a *queue,* or pigtail, to represent a horse's tail. The stereotypical 19th-century image of Chinese with shaved foreheads and pigtails is actually the result of a degrading dress code enforced by foreign invaders.

The 19th and 20th centuries did little to improve the reputation of foreigners. Between 1839 and 1860, the British launched a series of gunboat attacks, collectively known as the Opium Wars, against Chinese coastal towns in an attempt to force the Qing government to allow the open importation of opium. The Qing government had little choice but to submit to the foreign traders' demands, as it was preoccupied with what has been described as the bloodiest civil war in history. The Taiping Rebellion (1850 to 1864), was led by Hong Xiuquan, who had failed the imperial civil service examinations multiple times and, after suffering a nervous breakdown, finally claimed he was the younger brother of Jesus. This rebellion alone caused the deaths of anywhere from 20 to 50 million Chinese; thus suspicion of all things foreign, especially religions, was reinforced.

Later a coalition of Western powers divided China into economic zones of influence where many a Yankee blueblood family's fortune was made from the profits of exporting opium to China's estimated 2 million addicts.[2]

The Japanese joined the fray in 1895 and began annexing Chinese territory, culminating in full-scale invasion in 1937 and the notorious Nanjing Massacre that few Chinese have forgotten or forgiven.

Following WWII, both the U.S. and Russia

resumed their meddling, backing opposite sides in the Chinese Civil War between the Nationalists and the Communists, with the latter emerging victorious and the remnants of the Nationalists holed up on the island of Taiwan under U.S. protection ever since.

The consequence of such unsavory historical precedents has been a natural suspicion of foreigners and all things foreign; considering such a history, China may be forgiven for being a touch xenophobic.

■■■ MODERN ATTITUDES TOWARD FOREIGNERS

Most modern Chinese have never seen a foreigner. In the smaller cities and in the countryside, you may attract crowds of people who will stop what they're doing and stare at you. This should not be interpreted as being threatening or rude. It is just that the sight of a foreigner is so rare that you may become something of a local oddity (or celebrity, depending on how you look at it). Many Chinese view foreigners with a certain awe and fear, but the vast majority will nevertheless treat you with polite respect. In the large cities and areas where you are likely to be doing business, this reaction is becoming less common, but if you are invited to the countryside, you may find yourself the center of curious attention.

True Stories: Trade Wars

In 1793, the English envoy Lord McCartney arrived in China, seeking from the Chinese Emperor Qianlong an opening of trade. Replying to the request, the emperor wrote the King of England a message that read: "There is nothing we lack, as your principal envoy and others have themselves observed. We have never set much store on strange or indigenous objects, nor do we need any more of your country's manufactures."

Because of China's attitude toward foreign goods, British traders were forced to pay silver for Chinese exports that were in much demand. However, the drain on the silver-backed treasury was threatening the economic health of Britain. Although opium addiction was relatively unknown and importation was illegal in China, British traders began smuggling cheap opium from India into China, where it created an epidemic of opium addiction. In an attempt to stop illegal smuggling, the Chinese government seized several British opium ships and burned their illicit cargos. The British used this to justify sending gunboats to China, forcing the Chinese government to allow British traders free rein to import what they pleased, exempt from prosecution under Chinese law.

Many Chinese believe foreign visitors to be wealthy. Since it is usually only those with the time and money who can travel internationally, something beyond the economic ability of most Chinese, this perception is reasonably correct. However, it may occasionally cause some to feel envy and resentment.

■■■ HOW THE CHINESE VIEW OTHER NATIONALITIES

Many cultures hold common perceptions about foreigners that are shaped by their respective histories. The political correctness of Western countries has yet to penetrate Chinese culture and you should not be surprised to encounter attitudes that would seem prejudiced in the context of a Western boardroom. While it is of course inaccurate to generalize and say all Chinese share identical opinions, the following are some common attitudes toward foreigners.

Americans

Americans are often seen as open, warm, friendly and trusting, yet a little naive, especially when it comes to doing business in China. American society, compared to China's, is seen as shallow with little history or culture to boast of. In addition, the stereotype of the "ugly American" is well established, with Americans often viewed as brash, arrogant, boastful, and pushy, as well as impatient and lacking in self-discipline.

British

The British are reasonably well regarded, despite the rather sad history of their colonial occupation of China. They are thought to be clever and somewhat sophisticated, at least as foreigners go. On the negative side, they have a reputation for being cold and aloof, especially in Hong Kong, where British traders and officials often looked upon the Chinese as inferior colonials. This aloofness inhibits the development of close personal relationships with Chinese, which, as we know, is counterproductive to doing business in China.

Australians

Australians are regarded as being benign, but like Americans, often abrasive and lacking in sophistication and culture. However, Australians tend to be trusted as they are thought to be honest and forthright. Individual Chinese can usually develop a closer relationship with an Australian than with, say, an Englishman.

Canadians

Canadians are thought to be warmer than the British and less arrogant than the Americans, and more sophisticated than the Australians. Canada's good reputation is in large part due to the humanitarian efforts of the Canadian surgeon Dr.

Henry Norman Bethune, who is the only Westerner to have a statue in Communist China and
to have a hospital and a medical school named
in his honor. Originator of the Mobile Army
Surgical Hospital (MASH), Dr. Bethune's heroic
efforts treating wounded Chinese soldiers during
their battles with the Japanese were the subject
of writings by Mao Zedong that are now required
reading for all Chinese schoolchildren.

Japanese

The Japanese are thought of as hardworking, efficient, successful, and extremely loyal to their firms
and to Japan. Japanese success at adapting Western
technology is greatly admired. On the negative side,
because of the legacy of the Japanese occupation during WWII they are often seen as cruel, domineer-
ing, and untrustworthy. This lack of trust is partly due
to the excessive forms of politeness encountered in
Japan. Outwardly, Japanese are expected to appear
gracious and agreeable while nevertheless working
in their own best interests. This often causes them
to appear duplicitous. China also feels that Japan has
not adequately compensated its victims, or apolo-
gized enough, for its wartime actions, so there is still a
strong grudge held against them.

Curious Facts: Tai-Pan

James Clavell's popular novel about early Hong Kong traders, *Tai-Pan*, has brought this term into common usage. A "Tai-Pan" was an influential foreign businessman doing business in China or Hong Kong in the 19th century. Tai-Pan literally means "Big Class," which is equivalent to the English term "Big Shot." The name was used to refer to high-powered business executives and entrepreneurs in Hong Kong when it was still under British control. Originally used to designate those in charge of major companies such as Jardine Matheson, it is now used in a more general sense for business executives of any origin. Both this term and "Fragrant Grease" (bribes) are practically unknown outside of Hong Kong. The term Tai-Pan actually means head of a brothel (the correct Cantonese word is *loh-pan*). The early China traders misunderstood the meaning and adopted the term Tai-Pan, much to the amusement of the Chinese. Any foreigner applying the term to himself today would be viewed as a *poseur extraordinaire*. Should any of your Chinese partners refer to you as Tai-Pan they would be mocking you rather than praising your business acumen.

Koreans

The Koreans are viewed in a slightly more favorable light than the Japanese and are regarded as a stubborn people, but harder working than the Chinese. The Japanese used Korean auxiliaries during the war, and their perceived collaboration has tainted the Koreans in the eyes of many Chinese.

Overseas Chinese

Most Westerners would assume that overseas Chinese and compatriots from Hong Kong and Taiwan would have a greater advantage on the mainland than Westerners, but surprisingly this is rarely the case. Overseas Chinese are the proverbial "rich relations" both envied and disdained, as is common in many families. They are accused of having too much money, of flaunting it, and of being condescending to the more frugal locals. Many overseas Chinese have reported that antagonism toward them has increased since the mid-1990s. Showing off their wealth has also attracted the attention of criminal gangs, pickpockets, and robbers, who target them rather than non-Chinese Westerners.

Part of the problem lies in the clash of different business styles in places such as Taiwan, Hong Kong, and Singapore, and in what the overseas Chinese learn while abroad. This is further reminder of the wide diversity of practices within the seemingly homogenous Chinese culture.

■■■ CRIME AND CORRUPTION

Travel in China as well as Hong Kong, Taiwan, and Singapore is safer than in most U.S. cities. Street crime in these places is low and most Westerners in any case are immune, since local criminals know that a crime against a foreigner is more likely to get more attention from the police and the media. Tourism and international trade are now the lifeblood of China's economy, so scaring away visitors is bad for everyone's business. Any thug committing a crime against a Western business person will have both the police and the local crime boss to answer to.

Organized crime exists in China as it has for thousands of years, but it is unlikely that a Westerner will have any dealings with the mob, except possibly as a silent and perhaps unwitting partner in some company he or she is doing business with. (See "Loan Sharking," below.)

The really serious crimes occur well out of sight and involve mainly drug and human trafficking.

The Chinese worry least about violent street crime or robbery, and the majority of crimes they confront are minor theft and pick-pocketing.

The greatest concern reported by both Chinese and Western business people, however, is government corruption. Government and corruption seem to go hand-in-hand the world over, and as China's prosperity has increased so has the number of corrupt officials.

The current communist system in China is not unlike fascism as defined by Mussolini: "*Fascism should more appropriately be called Corporatism because it is a merger of state and corporate power.*" The state in China's case is the Communist Party itself. The wealthiest families are mostly old-time Party members; the most successful entrepreneurs, the sons and daughters of old Party members.

There is scarcely a business deal made in China without a member of the Communist Party, either on a village, city, provincial, or state level, taking a cut of the action. Somewhere, some Party boss is going to be in on the deal. Anyone who does not wish to hand over a piece of his business to the local Party boss would risk having his business license revoked, his bank account seized, and even his home and possessions confiscated by the state.

This style of corruption has been the real inspiration behind many anti-government demonstrations, from Tiananmen to the recent Hong Kong protests. The Chinese government, recognizing this, has recently made a big show of cracking down on certain corrupt officials who have profited from the close relationship between the party and business leaders. It remains to be seen if this will have a lasting effect on

True Stories: The Helpful Shopkeeper

While staying in Kowloon Robert went to the corner convenience store for milk. Not knowing the language, he went through a pantomime with the shopkeeper, "Do… you…have…milk?" Robert would use his hands to mimic milking a cow while saying the word "milk."

The shopkeeper looked bewildered.

Robert placed his fingers to his head in imitation of a cow's horns. The shopkeeper shrugged his shoulders and shook his head.

In a final attempt to get his meaning across Robert cupped his hand under his breast to represent a mother breast-feeding her baby. He then imitated a cow: "Mooo?"

Ah ha! The shopkeeper nodded knowingly and beckoned Robert to follow him. They went through the store and out the back into the alley, across a street, and into another alley, then into another building, up a flight of stairs, and down the hall where the shopkeeper winked and opened the door. Inside, sitting on couches, were a number of scantily clad young women.

"Moo" sounds very much like "Nue" which means "woman." Mistaking Robert 's "Moo for "Noo" and his pantomime of cupping an imaginary breast explains the storekeeper's earnest misinterpretation.

corruption, or is more about power consolidation and political gamesmanship among top party figures.

Very few of these activities will ever be visible

to the Westerner. It is highly unlikely that you will be directly approached by a government official seeking kickbacks and bribes, but know that your Chinese partners may well be, and in order to smooth over a deal, the cost of the bribe will be hidden in the expense budget or bid you receive. (See "Bribes," page 144.)

Prostitution

In the first edition of this book, prostitution in mainland China was almost nonexistent, largely underground and strictly confined to the Chinese themselves. The massage parlors, barber shops, hostess clubs, and room-service escorts were restricted to Hong Kong and Macau, where they are legal, and Taiwan, where they are ignored. Since then, the oldest profession has become a booming industry, expanding into all the traditional channels, from street prostitution to Internet escort sites.

In the late 1990s, prostitutes that worked the bars in the Beijing and Shanghai entertainment districts were limited to offering manual pleasuring under the table or in the back alley. If you tried to bring a hooker to your hotel room the hotel staff would alert the authorities. Since then everything has changed. Criminal penalties for both prostitutes and customers are severe by Western standards, but prostitution has nevertheless exploded; most current estimates have 20 million women involved in the trade.

Recent media reports reveal that prostitutes are now quite common even in five-star Western hotel chains, something unheard of ten years ago. Prostitutes can also be found at hostess bars and massage parlors, through on-line escort services, and even out walking the street.

If you the Western male business traveler receive an 11 pm phone call from the front desk asking if you are interested in a massage, your hunch is correct; they mean, do you want a prostitute sent to your room?

Despite all this, prostitution is still illegal in mainland China and mostly illegal in Taiwan, where there are a half dozen officially licensed brothels that are legal and hundreds of unlicensed brothels that are not. Enforcement of anti-prostitution laws depends on political machinations and organized crime relationships. A brothel may openly run for years without incident, only to be raided by police with full media coverage to produce some political impact, and then open the very next day, business as usual. In recent years the party has talked big about fighting prostitution. So while there will continue to be headlines about the government cracking down on vices like prostitution, brothels are nevertheless here to stay.

Drugs

Starting in the 1830s and continuing into the early 20th century, both China and the Chinese immigrant communities in North America had a notorious reputation for opium addiction. In the Chinatowns throughout the Western world could be found the proverbial opium dens with rows of cots on which men languidly smoked from long, thin opium pipes.

Opium had been used by Chinese doctors since ancient times as a pain reliever, but widespread use of the narcotic in the late 19th century was the result of a trade war. The British East India Company, in collusion with several trading firms from the United States, sought to balance their trade deficit by illegally exporting cheap opium from their plantations in India to China. Working with corrupt Chinese officials and criminal gangs, the scourge of addiction quickly spread throughout China, and the trade deficit soon reversed in favor of the West. China's rulers' attempt to put an end to the smuggling was met with British gunboats that used their superior technology to shell several coastal cities until eventually the Chinese government removed its prohibition against the importation of opium and even ceded Britain the island of Hong Kong.

Opium addiction was finally eradicated under Communist rule, and since the 1950s, until recently, drug use of any kind was virtually unheard of among the Chinese.

With the increase in wealth and the influence of Western culture, drug use is making a comeback in China. The drug of choice is no longer opium but methamphetamine. As in Japan and Korea, meth is favored for several reasons. It is cheap, and its ingredients are manufactured in China and easy to procure. Meth has a longer high than cocaine or opium, and it gives you more energy. This is why it is popular with long-haul truck drivers who work 24-hour shifts and factory workers who have to spend 12-hour shifts standing on their feet. The sad truth is that meth is the ideal drug to keep people functioning under inhuman working conditions, another of the hidden costs behind China's economic miracle.

While its increase among the working class is a result of harsh working conditions, drug use among China's new generation of spoiled rich kids is a result of Western fashion.

In the techno discos and night clubs of Shanghai, Beijing, and Shenzhen recreational drug use is increasing among the sons and daughters of wealthy entrepreneurs and industrialists. Cocaine and Ketamine have become symbols of wealth with a Western avant-garde cachet.

It is unlikely you will ever encounter illicit drugs

in China, but bear in mind that under China's criminal code, drug trafficking is a capital offense punishable by execution and drug users may be sentenced to long stretches in a rehabilitation camp.

Gambling

The one addiction many Chinese are prone to is gambling. There is scarcely a Chinese family that can't recount a story of an uncle or cousin who gambled his life's work away and impoverished his family.

Gambling is illegal in mainland China and Taiwan. Macau, the former Portuguese colony, has been allowed to continue its long-time gambling operations under the government's "One Country, Two Systems" policy and is known as the Las Vegas of Asia, complete with family theme parks and lavish casinos. Taiwan is proposing to set aside one of its many coastal islands as a special economic zone in order to build gambling casinos and get in on the lucrative tax revenue, and many say it's only a matter of time before China follows suit.

Though still illegal, gambling takes place in card and mah-jong parlors, on street corners, in underground casinos in the cities, through unofficial lotteries in the countryside (see Numbers Racket), and on hundreds of websites catering to Internet gamblers.

China's government hasn't formulated a plan to

deal with the increasing numbers of gambling addicts, and its approach so far has been to treat underground casino owners under anti-corruption laws and addicts as mental patients requiring treatment in one of their old Soviet-style re-education centers. This approach has only driven the trade deeper underground and left gambling addicts without any recourse to counseling or treatment like our twelve-step programs. But there is some movement toward bringing awareness of gambling addiction to the forefront and finding more benign ways to treat it. An emergency help line is now available for gambling addicts to call.

As a Western business traveler you will probably never be invited to any of the posh underground casinos (the experience is not unlike something from a James Bond movie). You may be invited to a friendly wager on the golf course, or a drinking game, to which prudence would be the recommended response.

Loan Sharking

Most of us associate usury and loan sharking with unsavory payday-loan shops or criminal organizations like the Mafia. Throughout China's long history, loan sharks have been ruthless, destructive, and ever present. During good times loan sharks would prey on the compulsive gamblers, making sure that after the gaming joints had taken their share the sharks would take whatever was left over. During hard times, especially during droughts and crop failures, loan sharks would move out into the countryside, offering starving farmers a loan to buy enough seeds for next season's planting, demanding the farmland as collateral. If the drought continued, within a year the loan shark would own most of the county and the farmers and their families would be left to starve along the side of the road. Many families had to sell their daughters into prostitution and their sons and wives into slavery to pay their debts.

Loan sharking, like the other vices, has made a comeback and is booming in what recent estimates say is a $630-billion-a-year industry. Interest rates charged on these loans are catastrophic, from 40% to 70%. This resurgence is due both to China's economic growth and China's banking system.

Banking in China has been, for as long as anyone can remember, a strict, tyrannical, and humorless enterprise. Twenty years ago if you wrote a check that was returned due to insufficient funds, the bank would immediately suspend your account, ban you from opening another account anywhere for five years, and send police detectives to your home or workplace to ask embarrassing questions.

Today China's banks are only slightly less difficult to deal with. The big banks prefer to lend to big corporations with ties to the Party, leaving small- and medium-sized business out in the cold. Even with proper credentials, getting a loan at a bank takes months, requires taking people out for dinner and karaoke, and waiting for approvals from different managers who all need to be "entertained"—and even then there's no guarantee.

Enter the loan sharks to provide the funding behind big property developments and new businesses and factories. Should any of these ventures fail, the properties will be stripped and the company executives kneecapped. It is not uncommon for dozens of business owners to suddenly disappear whenever a factory closes down or a real estate development fails to sell out. Most are thought to be hiding from loan sharks.

For you, the Western business person, knowing about this problem will help explain some of the strange behaviors you may encounter. Be wary when a company you are dealing with brings in a quote well under its competitors' or guarantees results no one else will. Such promises are seldom fulfilled, their only purpose being to secure a purchase order to use to stave off the loan collectors just a little longer. It is essential that you do credit background checks on any company you plan to deal with.

Networking

If you are limited in your own strength, then borrow the strength of the enemy. If you cannot neutralize an enemy, borrow an enemy's knife to do so. If you have no generals, borrow those of the enemy.

Sun Tzu, *The Art of War*

The first thing you need to do before you begin planning your trip to China is find a Chinese partner who can represent you and act as an intermediary to arrange your schedules and meetings with the correct people. It would be impossible for a Westerner to negotiate a deal in China without a (preferably) well-connected intermediary, known as *zhongjian ren* (the Middle or Intermediary Person).

Working with a Chinese partner is essential since the Chinese do not like to do business with complete strangers and will rely on go-betweens to make initial contacts. Whenever possible, try to use established relationships or an intermediary known by both sides to make the first contact. The intermediary should also be able to accompany you to your meetings and act as an interpreter.

Foreign companies doing business in China for the first time typically employ the services of local consultants to develop market strategies, conduct background checks, and identify potential investment partners, sales agents, and customers. More than 100,000 companies are active in the Chinese consulting industry, of which 65% are foreign firms that generate 85% of consulting industry revenue.[3]

So where do you find a reputable Chinese intermediary?

The China Business Information Center of the U.S. Department of Commerce can help Americans in arranging appointments with local Chinese business and government officials, and can identify the contacts they will have to establish. Most countries have similar government departments.

Another method is through third-party referrals from other companies that are already doing business in China. Large multinational law, accounting, and public relations firms with offices in China can often supply recommendations and even introductions to potential partners. You could also attend one of the

Curious Facts: Compradors

Throughout the 19th and early 20th centuries, Western traders who plied their trade between Hong Kong, Macau, and Shanghai overcame the obstacles of Chinese bureaucracy by employing a *comprador* (a Portuguese word; *maiban* in Chinese). A comprador was a Chinese or sometimes Eurasian who fulfilled the multiple roles of interpreter, broker, fixer, and accountant, all rolled into one. While a comprador was paid a salary by his Western employer, he also stood to earn considerable commissions by making backroom and side deals with suppliers, shippers, and distributors, as well as by using any insider information to cash in on stock market and real estate deals.

While the term comprador has gone out of use, the concept has not. Numerous business development and integration consultants fulfill the modern role of compradors for the Westerner looking to establish business connections in China.

Like the compradors of old, your Chinese intermediary may find opportunities associated with your enterprise to earn additional commissions. Most times, you will not be informed of them. Although from a Western perspective such side dealings would constitute a conflict of interest and breach of fair play, this is a given in Chinese culture.

many international business conferences and conventions that focus on East–West business opportunities.

At these conferences you will have the opportunity to meet China-based companies that are open to working with Western companies.

There are also dozens of companies that focus on acting as intermediaries, usually specializing in specific industries. Again, it is best to work from recommendations before choosing.

■■■ GUANXI

> *He who wishes to know the road through the mountains, must ask those who have already trodden it.*
>
> Chinese Proverb

Chinese society places immense importance on family and social relationships. This emphasis carries naturally over to business relationships as well. The word that describes this relationship is *Guanxi* (pronounced guan she) and broadly means "connections" but also refers to the amount of pull or influence a person wields.

Many of your activities in China will be aimed at establishing personal relationships with all the principals that you need to do business with. Although it is helpful for a Western manager to understand the necessity of establishing relationships and the role of Guanxi in Chinese society, it is best that your Chinese staff or intermediaries conduct the details of relationship building.

The complexities and nuances of Chinese culture preclude anyone other than the Chinese from understanding them all. However, the Chinese know this and make great allowances for foreigners. Your Chinese intermediaries will usually schedule meetings and dinners for you to attend, at which you are merely expected to play the genial guest, host, or presenter.

During social functions, the focus of your conversation should be in finding mutual interests outside of business. Talk about sports, music, literature, history, educational backgrounds, family, or well-known celebrities. The idea is to establish a personal relationship first. Once you have established a personal connection you can move to the next stage of negotiations and deal making.

Ideally, Guanxi is the creation of relationships based on reciprocity, mutual trust, and mutual benefit.

Guanxi is one of the first principles Westerners learn when they start to do business in China. It initially appears to be a simple matter of just getting to know each other first. This is deceptive. A rarely understood component of Guanxi is that it exists

True Stories: An Uncomfortable Silence

A meeting was arranged by a Chinese go-between for a Western executive and a Chinese business owner. Neither the Western executive nor the Chinese business owner could speak the other's language and there was no interpreter present. The business owner invited the executive into his office to have tea. The business owner poured the tea and toasted the executive, who returned the toast. They then sat in complete silence for some 20 minutes. Knowing better than to fidget or make any attempt at communication since it would have been futile in any event, the executive sat quietly and pretended to enjoy the tea. After 30 minutes of drinking tea in silence, the business owner stood up and thanked the executive for coming.

The executive was sure the meeting was a disaster since all they did was sit in uncomfortable silence. The next day, however, the Chinese go-between told the executive that the Chinese business owner was very impressed with the meeting and would like to arrange another to begin negotiations.

Why was the Chinese manager impressed? Many Chinese believe Western business people are impatient and lack self-discipline. Sitting quietly without either fidgeting or trying to make a pitch, the executive proved the expectation wrong.

in part as extra-judicial protection against dishonest practices. Chinese commercial legal codes and intellectual property rights were never fully developed in the past and remain weak to this day. Victims of fraud, embezzlement, and other criminal business practices may have little recourse in the legal system.[4] Look at it another way: would you be willing to hand over a substantial unsecured loan to someone you only had dinner with? Since your chances of recuperating your losses are slim, this is exactly what you could be doing when entering a business relationship. It would take more than a dinner and a couple of drinks to establish that kind of trust—nor should you be too eager to do so, since Guanxi is a sword that cuts both ways.

Guanxi was also an important element in gaining the cooperation of government authorities. In the past, attaining the needed government permits and licenses would entail being mired in a seemingly endless bureaucratic nightmare. You would have needed a friend who had "connections" in the government to move the paperwork through the machinery. Moving the machinery required "grease on the wheels": payoffs. Since there have traditionally been strict laws in China against bureaucratic corruption, with death sentences the norm for punishment, Guanxi was extremely important to ensure that the members giving and receiving bribes could be trusted.

Some of the old ghosts still haunt Chinese businesses, but like many cultural practices, the business of Guanxi is also evolving. With so many international companies doing business in China, and China's heavyweight entry into the fast-paced world of manufacturing and technology, the old snail's pace method of building trust is correctly being seen as hobbling growth and competitiveness. The trend toward contract-based business relationships over personal friendships will no doubt continue and the Chinese concept of Guanxi will come to resemble more the Western concept of networking.[5]

A final point to keep in mind is that Guanxi is a connection between individuals, not companies. Replacing long-time managers means that all the goodwill they instituted with your Chinese trading partners goes with them. The replacement will have to start the entire process again from scratch.

Despite the risks, efforts, and expense of playing the Guanxi game, it is a social obligation—like the company Christmas party—that you cannot escape.

■■■ INTERNET

Since the advent of the Internet some two decades ago, the Chinese government has sought to monitor and control how its citizens use it. From 2000 to 2008 the government implemented the Golden Shield Project, more commonly referred to as the Great

Firewall of China, which seeks to create a sealed-off Internet. Tens of thousands of government monitors and citizen volunteers collectively known as "Big Mama" regularly sweep through blogs, chat forums, and even e-mails to ensure nothing slips through that might challenge official state propaganda. Thousands of websites (many porn-related) are blocked outright, including any websites considered to be "dangerous to social security and public order." Destinations such as YouTube, Facebook, Flickr, and Wikipedia are blocked or heavily restricted.

Every post by a user with over 100,000 followers is automatically sent to Big Mama, and posts deemed harmful/illegal are deleted within five minutes. Special search engines remove keywords designated as harmful. Posters who have their posts deleted will soon have their accounts canceled as well.

All Internet users must use their real names and provide authentic government identification when registering an account, or their ISP risks losing its license. The vast majority of Chinese go online at Internet cafes and must likewise supply personal information in order to sign on.

Despite these efforts of the Chinese government to restrict and control what Chinese are able to access online, the more tech-savvy can circumvent the firewall and can visit restricted websites, though not without risks. Amnesty International notes that China "has the largest recorded number of imprisoned journalists and cyber-dissidents in the world." The "offenses" these prisoners are accused of include "communicating with groups abroad," "opposing the persecution of the Falun Gong," "signing online petitions," and "calling for reform and an end to corruption."

Needless to say, your Internet activity while you are in China will be monitored, so to avoid possible scrutiny by security agents, do not browse any of the above subjects when surfing. (See "Political Correctness," page 65.)

■■■ SOCIAL MEDIA FOR BUSINESS IN CHINA

In Taiwan and Hong Kong the popular social networking sites are the same as in the West, with Facebook, Twitter, and YouTube the most heavily used. Most give you the option of posting in English or simplified Chinese (used on the mainland). Since many Chinese can read English, posting to your Chinese business associates is an effective way to communicate.

On mainland China, Internet censorship blocks Facebook, Twitter, and most other well-known Western social media sites. LinkedIn has recently launched in China but must abide by strict guidelines. Facebook may follow.

The Chinese government fears that social media will be used to spread anti-government messages and organize protests. Its versions of the West's most popular platforms feature built-in spyware with restrictions on certain features, such as linking to unauthorized sites or joining chat rooms outside China. The following are some of the more popular social media sites within China for business.

Weibo

Weibo might best be thought of as China's Twitter, although this popular microblogging service provided users with video and picture functionalities well before Twitter ever did. For a period of time Weibo was the top platform for social discourse. Recent crackdowns on free speech by the government have caused some users to flee to other services.

QQ

QQ is a popular instant messaging service owned by the Chinese Internet giant Tencent. A messaging platform for the masses, QQ is one of the oldest messaging companies around, having been founded all the way back in 1999. In addition to chat, QQ also has a phone call function.

WeChat

Another mobile messaging and voice app owned by Tencent, WeChat, known as Weixin domestically, saw an influx of users from Weibo seeking a less public platform to communicate as well as to discuss and consume news. Like many other social media apps, WeChat and QQ are accessed overwhelmingly on smart phones.

Sites Like Facebook

A number of social networking sites resemble Facebook, including Renren, Pengyou, and Kaixin. But since they don't have nearly the number of users other social media sites do, they won't be essential for business communications.

■■■ BUSINESS ONLINE

While politics and religion are sensitive subjects online, business is not. At the end of 2014 China had 700 million Internet users with over 84% of them using mobile devices for access.

China now has the world's largest e-commerce market, with sales expected to reach $420 billion to $650 billion by 2020. In November of 2014, China's biggest annual shopping day smashed all records as online sales on Alibaba (China's much bigger version of Amazon) alone hit $9.3 billion and total sales exceeded $10 billion.

China is the first major market to develop in the post-Internet age. The old business model of first opening bricks and mortar shops followed by an on-line store has been reversed: many businesses open as online shopping sites and only open retail locations, if they ever do, after achieving their initial sales targets.

Currently a person or business can buy and sell both retail and wholesale and can pay or accept payments using a variety of safe and secure methods, including all major credit cards, PayPal, and Western Union. For the small entrepreneur this means you can now source and have manufactured products shipped directly from China without ever having to visit there in person. One caveat: Chinese still prefer to do business in person, and without on-site inspections and visits to insure you are getting what you ordered, you may have problems with your final product.

■■■ MOBILE PHONES

After mobile phones entered the Chinese market, they quickly became must-have status symbols. Current estimates give 1.2 billion mobile phone users in China, growing at a pace of 12 million per year. It is predicted that in the next five years over 90% of people age six or older will own a mobile phone in China.

Many U.S.- and Canada-based cell phones do not work in China. The few that do tend to be extremely expensive, so be sure to check with your provider on its overseas rates for China to avoid being hit with a mobile phone bill bigger than your hotel bill.

In order for a cell phone to work in China, it must be a GSM phone having the 900 as well as the 1800 MHz frequency or band. Some cell phone models, usually called "quad bands," have the international 900/1800 bands.

Provided your phone is not "locked" and is able to work in China, your next cheapest option is to install into your phone a Chinese SIM card that can be purchased at a cell phone or convenience store. You can then sign up for an account with China Mobile or China Unicom (the top two major wireless providers) or get by with prepaid phone cards available from newspaper kiosks and cell phone and convenience stores. Be aware that when using China Mobile to download information from the Internet the charges are quite high compared to other parts of Asia.

Most U.S. and Canadian carriers "lock" their handsets. This means that their phones will only accept their SIM cards. Some U.S. carriers will unlock your handset upon request (but not if you have an iPhone). Canadian carriers will not unlock your phone under any circumstance. There are numerous phone and electronic shops in every big city in China that can unlock your phone for small fee.

The cheapest and easiest alternative to buying SIM cards and unlocking phones is to simply buy or rent a handset and then use a pay-as-you-go SIM card from one of the Chinese carriers such as China Mobile. Unicom is the other carrier in China, and, while its coverage is decent, it is nowhere as broad as China Mobile's. When buying a SIM card be sure to ask whether the card allows you to call outside China. Some SIM cards allow it, others don't.

Chinese etiquette frowns on interrupting someone when he or she is speaking, especially during a business meeting, but the cell phone is exempt from this rule. Business people will all have their cell phones turned on and will interrupt you or stop speaking to answer every call that comes in.

■■■ THE PARTY LINE

> *The Northerners seek power so that they can become wealthy; the Southerners seek wealth so they can become powerful.*
>
> Chinese Aphorism

With its booming industries, opulent hotels, and adoption of Western styles, it is easy to forget that China has a Communist government. While special industrial sectors and free-trade zones conduct business according to free enterprise principles, the collectivist way of thinking still prevails. Privately, businesses have free reign to conduct their business as they see fit; publicly, each business must tout the Communist Party line.

It is therefore important to make sure your presentations and negotiations do not inadvertently contradict Communist Party doctrine. Current political correctness can change depending on unseen political machinations, so to be on the safe side focus your presentation on your corporate profile and avoid any economic or political theories such as espousing the benefits of free-market capitalism, Western-style efficiency, or democratic principles. Such comments may be interpreted as veiled insults by implying that the Communist system is inferior.

Avoid telling any stories of your experiences in Taiwan when on the mainland and vice versa. Since 1948, the island of Taiwan has been ruled by a separate "Nationalist" government opposed to the Communist government of China. The mainland has sought to bring Taiwan under its control, through the use of force if needed, while many in Taiwan are in favor of a separate status from the mainland. The debate has been a hot topic and there are sensitivities on both sides of the strait, so it is best to voice no opinions on the subject lest you insult one or the other. If somehow you let Taiwan slip into a discussion, it would be best to follow up quickly and reiterate that the Taiwan matter is an internal one, to be settled without outside (i.e. foreign) intervention. As a rule however, it's best not to discuss politics—not in public, and not in private.

Curious Facts: The "Brother of Jesus"

In recent years human rights groups have accused China of religious persecution against the Tibetan Buddhists, Muslim Uighurs, and the Falun Gong—a cult-like movement based on a mixture of ancient Taoist and modern New Age practices. Chinese governments have a long history of mistrust of, and animosity toward, religious movements, and for good reason. Religious cults have been the breeding grounds for numerous insurrections, the most recent being instigated by a man who claimed to be the reincarnated younger brother of Jesus Christ.

During the decline of the Qing dynasty (1644–1912), power was slipping from the hands of the decadent emperors to the palace eunuchs, and aristocratic families began carving out small kingdoms for themselves. The bureaucracy had become an old-boy network of corruption and payoffs. Opium addiction had grown into a

■■■ POLITICAL CORRECTNESS

In the past under Mao Zedong and especially during the Cultural Revolution political correctness was a matter of life or death. A political viewpoint that was one day official policy could the next day be condemned as counter-revolutionary, and anyone known to have supported it previously could be sent to re-education centers or outright shot as a traitor.

Political correctness in China does not extend to those areas that are considered especially sensitive

---

monstrous problem with large criminal organizations that grew fat from the profits of drug dealing and the accompanying ills of gambling, loan sharking, and prostitution.

Strange religious cults began to flourish. The Taiping Rebellion (1850–64) was a peasant uprising led by Hong Xiuquan, a poor, uneducated farmer who had learned the rudiments of Christianity from Protestant missionaries. Believing that he was the brother of Jesus Christ he preached a mishmash of Christian, Islamic, and Buddhist doctrines. Hong raised a large ragtag peasant army that succeeded, to everyone's amazement, in overcoming the imperial forces and seizing control of two-thirds of China. The Qing armies were able to defeat the Taipings only with the help of European mercenaries. Estimates of the death toll during the fourteen-year reign of Hong Xiuquan range from 20 to 50 million.

in the West, such as racism, sexism, and homophobia. You will occasionally see or hear depictions of other people or groups that would be utterly unacceptable at home.

So the more limited PC rule of thumb for you in China is to never mention anything that can be seen as critical of the government or in favor of movements critical of the government. Current taboo topics include Nepal, the Falun Gong, the protests by Uighur Muslims, the Tiananmen uprising (which China insists never happened), human rights abuses, democracy, government censorship, Taiwan, the Senkaku Islands dispute with Japan, and the ever-present official corruption.

Homosexuality

Up until 1997 homosexuality was treated as a criminal offense in China (Hong Kong decriminalized homosexuality in 1991, Taiwan in 1998) and was listed as a mental illness.

Traditionally, Chinese have not viewed homosexuality as a sin or immoral in the Christian Fundamentalist sense. There are no Taoist or Buddhist condemnations of same-sex preference, but that does not mean that it's welcomed either. Homosexuality remains stigmatized throughout most of the country because it conflicts with the ancient tradition in

China that children must marry and continue the family line by bearing offspring. This is an aspect of ancestor worship but in reverse: If you have no descendants, then there will be no one to burn offerings for you after you're dead, and you will find yourself penniless in hell.

Most Chinese have nothing against gay people so long as their own kids aren't gay. No surprise that very few Chinese gays come out to their families.

The police no longer raid gay hangouts as they did in the 1980s and '90s, and today's cosmopolitan cities like Beijing and Shanghai now have LGBT communities, complete with support groups, bars, and an array of gay meeting places.

If you are a gay (or straight) Western executive doing business in China, your sexual orientation is very unlikely to come up in conversation, but if it does, the best strategy is to take the Chinese approach—don't ask, don't tell.

Introductions

*Let your words be few, and your companions
select; thus you will escape remorse and
repentance; thus you will avoid sorrow and
shame.*

Chinese Proverb

Chinese prefer to be formally introduced when meeting someone for the first time. This applies to meeting other Chinese as well as foreigners. This is why it is important to have go-betweens set up initial meetings, so they can also make the formal introductions. In a formal situation such as meeting business or government officials, the Chinese may express little emotion and even seem unfriendly. This is a social norm known as *shehui dengji* (social status) in which an excessive show of familiarity is viewed as a lack of self-discipline, and runs against the Confucian protocol of respecting a person's social standing. Mirror such behavior yourself and do not show overenthusiasm.

Always stand up when being introduced and remain standing throughout the introductions.

The traditional Chinese greeting has been to place the left hand over the right fist, bow, and shake your two hands as though you are about to roll the dice. It is also a formal way of saying thank you. This formality is rarely used anymore, and although the Chinese will nod or bow slightly as an initial greeting, it is best to wait for your Chinese counterpart to initiate the style of greeting. Avoid the formal Japanese-style bow-at-the-waist, which would be politically incorrect.

Although a bow is no longer used, the Chinese will still greet someone by bowing their head as a show of deference and respect. Eye contact is important, but avoid looking intensely or too long into a person's eyes as this can make Chinese men, and especially women, feel uncomfortable.

Shaking hands has now become a part of Chinese culture but is usually reserved for formal occasions to show respect to VIPs such as government officials or visiting executives. Like all handshakes, the grip should be firm, but not too strong, and brief, since Chinese, like other Asians, are uncomfortable with physical contact in public. (Although curiously, close friends of the same sex may hold hands in public without any homoerotic implications.) It is highly inappropriate for a man to touch a woman in public.

If you visit a school or workplace or attend a presentation, you may be greeted with standing applause as a sign of welcome. Although it may seem self-congratulatory, the proper response is to applaud as well. This is simply a form of greeting and, by clapping along, you are not applauding yourself, but merely reciprocating the greeting.

Respect for seniority is an important part of China's social fabric; this has been the case long before Confucius formalized it in his codices. Always acknowledge the most senior (eldest) person in a group first, even though that person may not be the decision maker or even a part of the negotiation team.

For Westerners, learning numerous Chinese personal names can become confusing, to say the least. One trick is to try to remember just the "family" name, or surname. In China however, the surname comes ahead of the family name. For example, in China John Smith would be referred to as Smith, John. If someone introduces himself or herself as Zhang Mingzi, then addressing him as Mr. or Ms. Zhang is proper. Women's names can be difficult to distinguish from men's names. Using the prefix "Miss" or "Ms." is acceptable since Chinese women seldom take on the husband's family name during business (the noun *tai tai*, "Mrs.," is used only in family situations). Never call someone by only his or her last name and, unless specifically asked, do not call someone by his or her first name.

Chinese who frequently deal with foreigners or travel abroad on business may use a Western name such as David or John. They may request that they be addressed by their English first name once a relationship has been established.

Do not use the term "comrade" in China. Aside from being an awkward anachronism (especially when spoken by a Westerner), it is also in today's China a slang expression for a homosexual partner.

Finally, avoid gestures involving your mouth as they are considered vulgar. When in public, avoid biting your nails or removing food from your teeth. However, blowing your nose with a handkerchief is acceptable.

■■■ BUSINESS CARDS

After the initial greeting, whether bow or handshake, the next step is the formality of exchanging cards. The Chinese are very fond of exchanging business cards, and with visiting guests, everyone present at meetings or presentations will expect to exchange cards with you, so bring a plentiful supply. Have special cards made up in advance where one side is English and the other is Chinese.

You should always include your professional title on your business card. In Chinese business culture, a primary purpose of exchanging business cards is to determine that person's status within his or her organization, so be sure to include any special titles, awards, or distinctions you and your company have acquired.

If possible, have your business cards printed in gold ink since gold is the color of prestige and prosperity. Avoid red ink (and do not use a pen with red ink) since this is used when severing ties.

Present a business card by holding the card out using both hands, then bow slightly when it is received from you. In Chinese society, to hand something of importance using only one hand is an insult that indicates you are not truly giving it wholeheartedly. Accept cards the same way, with both hands and a slight bow.

As a further courtesy, present your card with the Chinese side facing up so your host will not have to flip it over to read the Chinese writing.

When receiving a business card, do not just quickly slip it into your pocket unread. Even if all the writing is in Chinese, you should still make a show of examining it for a few moments. Slipping a business card into your pocket without reading it is impolite.

∎∎∎ SAVING FACE

> *There are three great maxims to be observed by*
> *those who hold public situations; namely, to be*
> *upright, to be circumspect, to be diligent. Those*
> *who know these three rules know that by which*
> *they will ensure their own safety in office.*
>
> Chinese Proverb

One of the most important concepts underlying Chinese business and cultural etiquette is one we have all heard about: *mianzi*—face. Face is similar to the West's idea of reputation, a measure of one's status within one's social set. Having "face" means you are respected by your peers.

While the concept of face may seem quaint, do not underestimate its importance in social situations. In Chinese business culture a person's career depends on his or her reputation and social standing. One of the worst insults you could hurl at a Chinese is "You have 'lost face!'" or even worse, "You have 'no face' at all!"

The traditions surrounding face are the basis for most Chinese etiquette and reflect the importance of social acceptance and harmony among the Chinese. Unlike Western traditions of individualism, Chinese were for thousands of years dependent on the support of their community to survive; the more a person was accepted by his or her community, and the greater the reputation among that community, the better that person's chance of survival. This is partly because of geography. Only about 12% of China's land mass is arable. Throughout China's history floods and droughts have been frequent and their impact severe. Famine and starvation decimated the population time and time again (which gave rise to the traditional Chinese greeting, "Have you eaten today?"). During famines, community cooperation and cohesion were essential if families hoped to survive. Face was essential to survival, since anyone who developed a reputation for not fitting in would be ostracized and thus doomed.

As a foreigner, you will be forgiven slight offenses concerning face. Chinese do not expect foreigners to understand all the nuances of their culture and are therefore quite tolerant of most breaches of etiquette. Simple forms of politeness will suffice to prevent any serious embarrassment that would cause you to "lose face." But the more familiar you are with the customs surrounding face the better off you will be.

In the West, occasional disagreements, criticisms, and complaints are seen as minor slights and quickly forgotten. But in China, failing to appreciate face can cause serious problems. While a Western business person might be respected back home for being frank and a "straight-shooter," he or she would likely be viewed in China as unsophisticated and rude.

Causing the loss of face can create a lifelong enemy who will work secretly to exact revenge through sabotage and backstabbing. If you caused, inadvertently or not, the company you are doing business with to lose face, you might as well go back home.

Saving face is also the source of much misunderstanding over truthfulness in communications between Western and Chinese businesses. For the Chinese, saving personal face or the face of the managers and company is more important than admitting mistakes. For example, you may call your Chinese supplier to see how your order is coming along. The factory may have had some machinery breakdown because the head engineer failed to maintain the equipment, and production is now two weeks behind schedule. But to admit this to a client would entail losing face for the engineering department and for the company as a whole. So you will be told everything is moving according to schedule. Then when your order is late and you call to see what the delay is, you will be told that the shipping company was late in picking up the order.

For Western businesses this would be unacceptable; people are expected to own up to their mistakes and fix the problem. In China, however, face trumps truth, and if the truth has to be adjusted for the benefit of the community or the employees of the factory, then so be it.

How to Avoid Causing the Loss of Face

First, never criticize another employee or colleague in front of his or her peers.

Second, avoid the playful teasing that is common among Western coworkers. This is not a part of Chinese office culture, and many do not understand the joking nature and will take it as an insult.

In addition avoid the following:

- Calling someone out on a lie.
- Not showing proper deference to elders or superiors.
- Turning down an invitation with an outright no (see "The 'No' Word," page 101); always make some excuse such as "I would love to, let me check my schedule and I'll get back to you" or "I need to discuss it with so-and-so first."
- Being late without a really good excuse.
- Interrupting someone while they are talking.

- Being angry at someone—mutual loss of face for both parties.

- Revealing someone's lack of ability or knowledge (such as not being able to speak English).

How to Give Face

To give someone face, praise him or her for doing a good job in front of their peers or superiors. By giving someone face you earn respect and loyalty. The maxim "Praise in public, criticize in private" is a good guideline. Additional ways of giving face include:

- Giving high marks on customer evaluation forms.

- Treating someone to an expensive meal or banquet (the most popular face-giving technique and almost *de rigueur* after cementing business deals).

- Giving sincere compliments and showing that you're enjoying your company when being entertained.

- Giving an expensive gift, especially an imported one.

■■■ THE CHINESE AND WOMEN

A virtuous woman is a source of honor to her husband; a vicious one causes him disgrace.
                                        Chinese Proverb

According to Confucius, women are secondary to men. They were expected to obey first their fathers, then their husbands, and during widowhood, their sons. In the past, marriages were arranged, and a woman's duty was to remain married and bear children, preferably sons. Divorce was not allowed, nor was remarriage by widows. Conversely, even up to the early 20th century, wealthy men could keep as many wives as they could afford. Essentially, women were chattel.

In the past fifty years, China has gone a surprisingly long way toward improving the status of women, but Chinese women are still far from having achieved equal rights with men. In business, women have the status of "honorary" men. Proper etiquette toward Chinese businesswomen is no different from etiquette that is directed toward businessmen.

If you are a man, avoid anything considered flirtatious such as compliments on looks or dress. Avoid prolonged eye contact and any physical contact. As mentioned previously, it is difficult to distinguish Chi-

True Stories: No Card, No Face

A Western executive arrived for the first time in China without business cards. He was told that in China he could have cards specially made and printed in both languages and that they would be ready the next day. Unfortunately, that very night he was invited to a welcoming dinner by the Chinese management team. When the senior Chinese manager introduced himself, he handed the executive his business card and then held out two hands expecting a reciprocal business card. When the executive explained his cards were not ready, the manager "lost face," an inauspicious first impression.

Why did the Chinese manager lose face? Even though neither party was at fault, because the manager had held out his hands expecting a business card, when the executive turned out not to have one, the manager caused the executive embarrassment, and thus, to lose face. Since the manager was also the host, his causing a guest to lose face resulted in *himself* losing face for not being a gracious host! A double-whammy!

nese female names, and married women usually retain their maiden names. The safest course is to address all Chinese women by their last name and add the prefix "Miss." For example, Wu Meili would be addressed simply as Miss Wu.

Foreign businesswomen should not experience any discrimination, but prejudice against "strong women" is deeply rooted in China. Women in China, whether on business or accompanying their business-man husband, should act and dress in a formal manner and essentially not draw too much attention to themselves. It is acceptable for women to smoke and drink alcoholic beverages at banquets and parties, but of course in moderation.

Meetings

*Whoever is first in the field and awaits the
coming of the enemy will be fresh for the fight;
whoever is second in the field and has to hasten
into formation will fight already exhausted.*

Sun Tzu, *The Art of War*

You will most likely rely on a Chinese intermediary
to arrange appointments and meetings. Most Chinese company officials will be able to communicate
in English, but it is best to bring your own interpreter,
if possible, to help you understand the subtleties of
everything spoken during meetings.

■■■ WHEN TO GO

In order to plan a fortuitous time to visit China, know
that the best months for scheduling appointments are
April to June and September to October.

Business and government hours are 8:00 AM to 5:00 PM, Monday through Saturday. There is, however, a five-day workweek in larger cities.

Store hours are 9:00 AM to 9:00 PM, daily. Most stores in the larger cities like Shanghai, Beijing, and Hong Kong, however, remain open until 10:00 P.M. Most Chinese workers take a break between 12:00 PM and 2:00 PM.

Times to avoid China for business are during the Golden Weeks: Chinese New Year, May Day, and National Day. Ghost Month (see below) is also not a good time to conduct business: it is a more subdued time, when thoughts turn to the family and to introspective contemplation, remembering one's ancestors.

Chinese New Year

Chinese New Year (also called Spring Festival in China) is celebrated on the twelfth month of the lunar calendar and usually falls somewhere between January and February on the Western calendar.

Spring Festival is arguably the most important holiday in China, when millions of people travel to their homes any way they can in order to visit with family. For many people, it is the only time during the year they can make such a trip, so it becomes the Chinese version of Thanksgiving and Christmas rolled into one.

During this time most businesses, factories, and government offices will be closed or run with a skeleton crew only. No business can be conducted during this time. During Chinese New Year, which can last up to a week, families perform numerous rituals to assure that the coming year will be auspicious. Cleaning the home symbolizes casting out clutter and dirt and cleansing the negative aspects of the past year. Then new clothes and new shoes are worn to usher in the New Year.

While shops and offices are empty, travel is hectic and crowded as family members return to their parents' homes for a special meal together on New Year's Eve. This is the largest meal of the year, much like Thanksgiving, and there must always be plenty of leftovers to symbolize that the New Year will start with plenty and ensure abundance throughout the year.

May Day and National Day

These holidays reflect China's socialist past, commemorating the workers on May 1, and the official founding of the People's Republic of China on October 1, 1949.

Ghost Month

Ghost Month falls on the seventh month in the Chinese calendar, occurring between July and September. Traditionally, Ghost Month is the time in which hell opens its gates and releases its ghosts and spirits to visit earth. The Mexican holiday Dia de los Muertos and our own Halloween have a similar mythology—a day in which spirits, fairies, and assorted ghosts are allowed one day on which they can return to the world of the living. The Chinese lord of hell, however, is much more generous and allows Chinese ghosts a whole month's vacation. This is the time of the Ghost Festival, when families prepare ritual offerings of food and burn paper money to please the visiting ghosts and spirits as well as deities and ancestors. Other activities include buying and releasing miniature paper boats and lanterns on water, which signifies "giving directions to the lost ghosts."

Despite the celebrations, with so many ghosts roaming about it is best not to engage in certain activities. Ghosts tend to be jealous of too much success and may jinx any business dealings. Activities and events such as weddings, special plans, moving, business deals, and travel are placed on hold until the end of the month.

■■■ MEETING ETIQUETTE

> *It is easy to convince a wise man, but to reason with a fool is a difficult undertaking.*
>
> Chinese Proverb

Punctuality is of major importance. Being late for an appointment is a serious insult in Chinese business culture so plan your itinerary with time to spare to account for the vagaries of Chinese transportation and traffic.

In accordance with Chinese business protocol, enter the meeting room in hierarchical order with the senior member entering first. The Chinese will assume that the first foreigner to enter the room is the senior executive of your delegation.

The most important member of your company or group should open and lead important meetings. The lead executive need not do most of the talking but can opt to moderate the presentation calling on lower-ranking associates to elucidate key points, with each presenter returning the chair to the lead executive.

During presentations, interruptions and questions of any kind from subordinates are considered inappropriate. Write down any questions you may have and bring them up at the end of the discussion.

Curious Facts: Lucky and Unlucky Numbers

Although publicly Chinese do not pay much credence to old superstitions, privately, most would still avoid unlucky days and numbers when doing business.

In China the unluckiest number is not 13, it is 4. The reason is that in both Mandarin and Cantonese, the number 4 is synonymous with the word for "death," the only difference being in the tone. This is why you will notice that elevator buttons jump from 3 to 5 and even from 13 to 15. Anything using the number 4, or combinations thereof, is considered unlucky, such as giving four of some item, or the number 4 on a house or apartment number. Conversely, the number 8 is a lucky number suggesting good fortune. At formal gatherings such as a dinner party or wedding dinner, each table is usually set for either eight, ten, or twelve people, with the latter being the most common.

The hierarchy within a Chinese organization is complicated. It is often difficult to identify who makes the final decision. Thus, treat everybody with equal respect and be prepared to present your material to many different people at varying levels of authority.

Speak in short, simple sentences free of jargon and slang. Pause frequently so that people will be able to understand everything you have said.

Finally, allow the Chinese to leave a meeting first.

■■■ BUSINESS ATTIRE

> *Spreading out pennants and making the flags*
> *conspicuous are the means by which to cause*
> *doubt in the enemy. Analytically positioning*
> *the fences and screens is the means by which to*
> *bedazzle and make the enemy doubtful.*
>
> Sun Bin

Dress styles are changing quickly in today's China. The uniform-like Mao jacket is rare in the larger cities and has been replaced by Western-style suits and, sometimes, ties. Foreigners should dress formally. In Chinese business culture, conservative suits and ties in subdued colors are the norm. Men should wear suits and ties to formal events (tuxedos, however, are not a part of Chinese business culture). Bright colors of any kind are inappropriate.

Women should likewise dress conservatively and avoid low necklines, hemlines that rise above the knee, high heels, and short-sleeved blouses. Revealing clothing on women is considered offensive to Chinese businessmen. Jewelry will be noticed, and since ostentation is frowned upon, do not wear overly expensive jewelry or showy ornaments. Unpretentious gold jewelry and a Swiss watch will often provide all the prestige required.

Casual dress should be conservative as well. Men and women can wear jeans; however, jeans are not acceptable for business meetings, and shorts should only be worn for exercise.

■■■ WEATHER

China spans many degrees of latitude, with wildly varying terrain and climate. It has a variety of temperature and rainfall zones, including continental monsoon areas. In the north, winters are cold and dry, summers short and hot. In the south, winters are rainy, while summers are hot and humid.

Find out what the weather conditions are for the region and season you are traveling in and prepare accordingly. As a rule, sensible shoes, and an umbrella, are essential for any sightseeing.

■■■ PRESENTATIONS

Modesty is attended with profit; arrogance brings on destruction.

Chinese Proverb

Because of the Chinese emphasis on communal decision-making, you will most likely have to make presentations to different levels and departments of an organization. Other members of the organization may sit in at the last minute, so be prepared by ensuring you have extra copies of your proposal.

Presentation materials of any kind should be only in black and white. In Chinese culture, colors have different meanings and you do not want to choose an "unlucky" color.

Prepare summary copies of your presentation, preferably in English and Chinese, and pass them out at the beginning of the meeting.

At the beginning of your presentation, it is customary to offer some kind words to the host, the company, and the country. Be sincere but do not overdo it. If you use an interpreter, try to ensure that he or she has the opportunity to study your presentation materials in advance of your meetings.

Contrary to the expressive hand gestures found in Western cultures, the Chinese rarely use their hands when speaking. Braggadocio, showmanship, or grand oratory gestures will only annoy your Chinese audience.

In Chinese business culture, humility is a virtue. Exaggerated claims will often be met with suspicion and you can expect any bluffs to be called.

Do not point your finger when speaking, since pointing is used when you are accusing someone of

Curious Facts: Lucky and Unlucky Colors

Colors play an important part in Chinese superstitions and when deciding on one's wardrobe a few colors should be avoided.

White is the color of death, and during traditional funeral ceremonies the mourning garments are plain white. Therefore, avoid wearing all-white dresses, suits, or shirt and trousers. This would be the Western equivalent of showing up at a business meeting dressed all in black. It is quite acceptable to wear a white shirt or blouse, but it is best to team it with pants, a skirt, or a jacket of a different color.

A traditional funeral rite is a gift of money often placed in a yellow envelope with a blue stripe, so leave the yellow-and-blue striped ties or scarves at home to avoid bad luck.

Red (with the exception of the color of your pen ink) is a very "lucky" color, and wearing some article of clothing that is red, such as a tie with a red stripe or a red scarf, will appear fortuitous. A woman wearing too much red, however, such as a red dress with matching purse and shoes, will look a bit silly, since an all-red outfit is what a bride traditionally wears on her wedding day.

wrongdoing. To point out something on a screen or model use an open palm, not your index finger.

For Westerners, looking people in the eye when talking is considered a show of honesty, attentiveness, and respect, while averting the eyes is considered a sign of deception. However, this is not the case in China. Steady eye contact is inappropriate, especially when subordinates talk with their superiors. As in many cultures, steady eye contact can sometimes be viewed as a sign of aggression or defiance. To avoid this, Chinese often talk while looking downward.

The safest approach is to make some initial eye contact and then only make eye contact occasionally thereafter.

Chinese business people usually rely on subjective feelings and personal experiences in forming opinions and making decisions. Keep this in mind during presentations and be sure to emphasize the human side of your business first and save the hard statistics for a follow-up meeting.

Exude sincerity and goodwill, but be firm and consistent in making your position clear. Be honest in your responses to questions, proposals, or criticism. If you sense something is amiss, or if there is any kind of misunderstanding, make sure you clear things up before proceeding further. The Chinese may have come to an understanding you did not intend to convey and it will be much more difficult to reverse their opinions later.

Sun Tzu (Sun Zi), author of *The Art of War* and China's legendary "father of military strategy," is the source for the famous "know your enemy" saying

True Stories: Snake Oil

On my first trip to China with a delegation of publishers, we visited a traditional Chinese medicine factory, where the local boss gave us an introduction into the wonders of Chinese medicine, with some extravagant claims about its efficacy. One crusty old man in our group listened, and then said in a rather gruff voice that he thought "it was all just a bunch of snake oil!"

Our translator carefully spoke in Chinese with the boss of the factory, who translated the boss's reply, "He assures me there are not any snakes in his products!"[6]

whose application is especially pertinent to business. Try to get a sense of the current social, economic, and political climate of China. One of the best ways to get the latest news is to talk with other foreign business people stationed in China who have more experience. In the larger cities, you can find associations, pubs, and clubs where foreign executives and embassy staff will gather. Spending a few hours buying drinks and picking the brains of the expatriates can produce better intelligence than a month of reading *People's Daily*. Social and political trends that can affect the way business is conducted come and go. One needs to be both knowledgeable and savvy enough to know when and how to adapt to changes in the Chinese environment.

■■■ ENGLISH

English is the world's de facto *lingua franca* of business and as a result, China may soon have the greatest number of English-speaking people of any country. Naturally, you cannot rely on English speakers always being present, so you should have a translator available for all presentations, negotiations, and discussions. Know that many Chinese study English and can understand more than they will reveal. Keep this in mind when discussing sensitive information with your fellow citizens in front of Chinese observers. Pretending not to understand English in order to glean information from those who drop their guard is a common tactic.

Remember to speak slowly and clearly, and pause at the periods. Avoid using colloquialisms, slang, or puns since these will cause confusion even when translated correctly into Chinese.

Corporate
Training

He who can suppress a moment's anger, may prevent many days' sorrow.

Chinese Proverb

Part of a presenter's job is to be a teacher. Understanding the differences in teaching styles is of some benefit. The Western style of teaching, known as the Socratic Method, encourages students to question and challenge the theory and the teacher. A large part of class time is devoted to open debate and question-and-answer sessions. This style of instruction is almost unknown to the Chinese.

China follows the style of Confucius where the teacher is the fountainhead of knowledge and the student's role is to absorb verbatim the teacher's instructions. In the educational system, teachers lecture and students dutifully take notes that they memorize in order to reproduce them during exams.

It can be unnerving for a Western manager training Chinese staff to face a wall of silence during question time. This does not signify that the audience has understood the material—usually quite the contrary. According to Chinese culture, asking a teacher a question implies a challenge to the teacher's credibility, as if the student did not trust the teacher's competence. It could also imply the teacher did an inadequate job of conveying his or her information. Unfortunately, the result is that students might not have understood your instructions and so cannot adequately carry out the given tasks. Often students will gather afterward to come to a consensus of what your presentation or instruction was really about.

To counteract this tendency and make communication easier, you should urge your audience at the beginning of each session to ask questions. Explain that you understand the cultural differences in teaching, but since you are a Westerner, it would be quite acceptable to ask questions and this would not offend you in any way.

Provide outlines of the material and distribute them in advance to give staff a chance to preview the topic and think of questions to ask.

Do not single people out for asking questions

("How about you?") as this puts them on the spot and can make them very uncomfortable when surrounded by their peers.

Whenever possible, present information in visual form. This helps to overcome the language barrier and plays to the Chinese tradition of graphic representation. PowerPoint-accompanied presentations are almost mandatory.

When demonstrating new technologies, emphasize hands-on training. Do not feel that it is patroniz-

---

True Stories: No Looky

I was an observer during a training session that was a part of the bank's MIT program for Chinese middle managers at its China headquarters. The corporate trainer was an Englishman who seemed to do a fine job in presenting their new procedure and wisely included some graphics and charts. The room of Chinese managers applauded after the presentation and, naturally, no one had any further questions. Afterward, I asked a couple of the Chinese managers what they thought of the presentation. Having previously established a personal relationship with them, I knew that I could expect an honest rather than politically correct answer. Although they never slandered the presenter—Chinese would never be so insulting toward a foreign guest—it was obvious that the entire Chinese management team thought the presenter to be a pompous ass. Much of this animosity first arose because the presenter never made

ing to repeat yourself when presenting a new concept, direction, or process. Use different sentence phrasing to repeat the same instruction.

International business innovation in China is very much technology driven, not business–model driven as in the West. Most Chinese managers will have engineering degrees, not MBAs. Any Western manager without a strong working knowledge of the technology used in his or her project will not fare well in China.

eye contact with his Chinese audience, which they in turn interpreted as arrogance on the Englishman's part.

Having a drink later with the presenter in an English-style pub I asked him about his use of eye contact during the presentation. He said one of the first pieces of advice he was given for presenting to a Chinese audience was: never look them in the eye. My guess is that he confused two separate principles and got both wrong. A common mistake novice presenters often make is to focus on only one or two people in the front row. The common advice is: do not just stare at the people in the front row, make eye contact with everyone in the room. The second piece of advice is to not stare overlong at another person, especially Chinese. The presenter's solution to both these problems was simply to not look at anyone. Hence the saying: a little bit of knowledge can be a dangerous thing.

Negotiations

To remain disciplined and calm while waiting for disorder to appear amongst the enemy is the art of self-possession.

Sun Tzu, *The Art of War*

■■■ TIME

Generally, for new business development, several trips to China will probably be necessary before the business contracts are finalized. Remember, the Chinese prefer to establish a strong relationship before closing a deal, so you need to be flexible with your scheduling in case negotiations drag on, and they will. Even after the contract is signed, the Chinese will often continue to press for a better deal. One reason for this lies again in history. Because of their long history and traditions, Chinese tend to approach business as a long-term enterprise. Get-rich-quick and fast-money deals are viewed with the skepticism they deserve.

Do not expect a fast agreement from the Chinese side. A basic Chinese military tactic often used in business is to stall the opponent until conditions favor your side. If you start to receive a seemingly endless litany of questions, requests for more information, and a variety of demands, you are probably the recipient of this tactic. Since each day you spend in a hotel is costing your company time and money, time is on the Chinese side.

To hurry up the process and provide you with some leverage, you need to start negotiations with several competing companies simultaneously. Ethical views on this multiple-pitch approach vary depending on the type of business, but it is one of the few plays you can make. If one company begins to stall you, leave them alone for a while and focus on the next. By not pressing the first company for a quick decision, they will suspect you are dealing with another company and may feel the need to move faster on the deal.

■■■ DECISION-MAKING

One of the often-noted differences between Western and Chinese business culture is in decision-making. A gross generalization has Western entrepreneurs making snap decisions while conservative Chinese managers plod along a methodical approach in which decisions are made by forming a consensus among the management team. Much has been written about the dichotomy between individual versus collective management styles in Western and Eastern cultures, but this is not to be taken too literally.[7] While a consensus among members of a Chinese team needs to be established, this is not always done through open and equal discussions and debates; rather, far from it.

The nail that sticks out gets hammered down is a famous Asian proverb. What it means here is that when a group of Chinese managers makes a decision, you cannot assume that everyone is in agreement, only that no nails are sticking out. The group decision can be arrived at by many variables, such as political correctness, family relationships, interoffice politicking, and seniority. The management team may agree to a course of action, but there can be many who are secretly against the decision and will work covertly to undermine the results, much to the bewilderment of Western managers, who are thinking everyone is on board.

While it is correct to treat everyone on the Chinese side as a team member, this is really a matter of giving everyone face. You may still need to convince each member individually afterward on a one-on-one basis. You also need to be shrewd enough to spot who the real power brokers are within a group and target them with special attention secretly and away from the group to avoid jealousies.

To provide everyone with face and show yourself to be the egalitarian leader you are, include the Chinese staff in the decision-making process by discussing the issue and asking others for their opinion, even though you are unlikely to receive anything other than a "Yes, very good!" This shows that you understand the pretense of the Chinese decision-making process so the staff will be more accepting and respectful of the final decision.

Finally, remember that many Chinese will want to consult with astrologers or wait for a lucky day before they make a decision.

■■■ THE "NO" WORD

Misunderstanding over the use of the word "no" is one of the most frequent causes of frustration in business negotiations. It is common knowledge that Chinese people do not like to say no.

In accordance with Confucian ideals of humility and service, Chinese do not like to disappoint someone or seem ungenerous or unhelpful. The Chinese consider it rude to say no to someone

True Stories: Panash

In the mid-'80s, a small bakery/coffee shop owned and operated by a Hong Kong department store had just closed and the Chinese manager was trying to think of ways to use the space. He wanted to keep the space as a bakery/coffee shop, since remodeling it would not be cost effective. As the manager stood there, he spotted something in the men's section of the department store. A nearby temporary display was advertising Panasonic electric shavers sold under the brand name Panashave.

The manager was looking at a large blue-and-white acrylic "Panashave" sign near the display and he mysteriously instructed a worker to cut the "ave" from the sign. Taking the sign back to the empty coffee shop, he proudly held the sign up: "Panash" it said. Never mind that it was a misspelled version of "panache"; it conveyed exactly the meaning and look for the coffee shop and bakery that the manager wanted.

Panash is now a successful chain of coffee shops and bakeries located throughout Hong Kong. This example of "on the fly" thinking perfectly captures the entrepreneurial spirit of many Chinese.[8]

even if that is the only answer possible. This cultural norm finds its most frustrating aspect in asking Chinese for directions. Should the person questioned not know what you are talking about, he or she will nevertheless give you false directions rather than appear unhelpful. Despite the wasted hours of wandering you may incur, remember they were simply being polite.

Likewise, in business the Chinese will not usually come out and say no to a proposal directly. Instead they will give a vague response such as "perhaps," "I'm not sure," "I'll think about it," or "We'll see"—all of which usually mean "no."

Another area in which the Chinese reluctance to say no can cause misunderstanding is in not admitting that they don't understand something. If you ask a Chinese student if they understood they would inevitably answer yes regardless if they did or did not. Unlike Western countries, where common wisdom holds there are no stupid questions, the Chinese have not been encouraged to express confusion.

This same approach transfers into the business world. Whenever a manager explains and assigns a task to a staffer, the typical response is "No problem," but actually, there may be problems and it is unlikely that you would hear about it. Proper etiquette is to avoid giving a negative response or information. The desire not to disappoint also manifests itself in technical perfectionism. The IT or engineering staff can delay a project because of their focus on trying to make everything technically perfect, and mire a project despite the deadlines.

To overcome these potential problems you need

to establish open communication with the staff. Explain that Western business practice allows for mistakes when working on new projects and that these are an accepted part of the learning curve. Make it clear that no one should feel embarrassed to bring you a bad report. Also, be sure you speak with not only project managers, but also the rest of the staff. As we learned earlier, giving everyone a chance to provide input helps build team loyalty and communication so you will be better able to gauge progress and anticipate problems.

■■■ CHINESE NEGOTIATING TACTICS

That an ancient Chinese treatise on military strategy has become almost *the* textbook for business negotiation seminars should be a heads up. James Clavell's novel *Noble House* portrayed Hong Kong traders as shrewd tacticians whose business edge was tempered by deep contemplation of Sun Tzu's *Art of War*. Clavell's novel did much to popularize *The Art of War* in the West, and it has spun off a whole genre of "military-texts-as-applied-to-business" books. Despite such shades of sinister esoteric knowledge, most Chinese negotiating tactics are quite commonplace and there is no need to re-educate yourself in the mold of a battlefield commander.

One useful piece of advice from the old general is: *Make your defense impenetrable, then wait for the enemy to make a mistake.* In negotiations, this means going in confident and prepared, doing the research and knowing your options, and then cultivating the patience needed to wait out your opponent.

The following are a few common negotiating tactics and possible ways to counter them:

Controlling the Meeting Place and Schedule

The Chinese know that foreigners who have traveled all the way to China will be reluctant to travel home empty-handed. Stalling negotiations until just before their scheduled return puts a lot a pressure on foreign executives to cement a deal usually by ceding further last-minute concessions.

COUNTERMOVE

Do not expect quick results, allow extra time for all activities, always assume an unhurried and nonchalant attitude toward signing deals, and be willing to cut your losses and go home. Let the Chinese side know that failure to negotiate a contract is preferable to making a bad deal.

Threatening to Do Business Elsewhere

A well-known tactic is to play competing companies off one another. The Chinese may threaten to approach rival firms if their demands are not met.

COUNTERMOVE

Fight fire with fire. If the going gets tough, you may let the Chinese side know that you have also made inquiries with other Chinese rival companies. If there are no other Chinese companies that offer the same service or product, then you can let it be known that your superiors are actually more interested in making such a deal with companies from a rival country such as Korea, Japan, Vietnam or Taiwan. This would play to national pride, and Chinese business people would generally be reluctant to lose a deal to a foreign competitor.

Using Friendship to Extract Concessions

Once personal relationships are established, the Chinese side may seek to take advantage by asking for further concessions as a personal favor and sign of friendship.

COUNTERMOVE

Avoid committing to further concessions by claiming that the parameters of the deal you negotiate were mapped out in advance, and any additional changes would need to be submitted to your superiors for approval. The Chinese cannot argue with that since it is in accordance with their own Confucian protocol of deferring to superiors.

Showing Anger

Contrary to the Confucian aversion to showing negative emotion, the Chinese side may put on a displayed show of calculated anger causing the foreign party to fear losing the contract altogether. Often this is worked in as part of a "Good Cop, Bad Cop" tactic.

COUNTERMOVE

Recognize such a display as the hardball tactic it is and remain unfazed.

Attrition

Chinese negotiators have been known to wear down foreign negotiators by various diversions and extended discussions. Taking clients out for a dinner, karaoke, and drinking games into the early hours of the morning before important meetings is a favorite tactic.

COUNTERMOVE

By preparing yourself and ensuring due diligence ahead of your trip, you will be better able to deal with unexpected developments and make smart decisions despite suffering from lack of sleep and a possible hangover. Treat your trip to China like a marathon race. Pace yourself accordingly. Follow the Confucian model of moderation in all things to help you stay sharp and unfrazzled during what is ordinarily an exhilarating but taxing experience.

Playing the Victim

Chinese may begin negotiations by showing humility and deference, often accompanied by stories of financial and business hardships. This is designed to present themselves as vulnerable and weak. You are therefore stronger, and *noblesse oblige* would require you to help them by making further concessions.

COUNTERMOVE

Know that wringing concessions, like street market haggling, is an expected part of the process. Be sure to insert a few unnecessary clauses and demands into the start of every negotiation then allow these to be "reluctantly" conceded.

■■■ CONTRACTS

Traditionally, Chinese commercial law was practically nonexistent and lawyers were considered, perhaps correctly, to be of a low status and dubious character. Deals were made on a mere handshake, and to bring a lawyer in to negotiate a contract was both an insult and a sign of devious intentions.

In order to do business internationally China is grudgingly enhancing its commercial legal codes and encouraging the use of written contracts, but old attitudes are hard to change. Written contracts are still

secondary to personal relationships between associates.* To the Chinese, to show up with a draft legal
contract is seen as inappropriate, the equivalent of
bringing a prenuptial agreement on a first date.

To appease anxious foreign executives who are
hoping to have something down on paper that they
can show the home office upon their return, Chinese executives may sign a "Letter of Intent"–style
contract. To the Chinese, this contract is not legally
binding and serves only as a list of useful talking
points. This could come as an unpleasant surprise
to the executive who already made a deposit on
his or her vacation home based solely on a written
contract.

In contract negotiations, a Western executive's
primary job is to discuss and come to an understanding verbally with his or her associate, then allow
subordinates or third parties to negotiate for further
concessions and work out the details later. Even after
the details have been hammered out and contracts
signed, the Chinese may still drag you back to the
negotiating table for more concessions. Remember
when negotiating to factor such additional costs into
your profit margin.

* However, Hong Kong and Taiwan have had a longer history working with
  international companies and understand the importance of contract law
  more than mainland Chinese currently do.

True Stories: The Hurried Executive

A story often told during happy hour at the expatriate haunts of China tells of the inexperienced American executive sent to China and given three days to negotiate a new contract with one of his company's suppliers. The welcoming committee of bubbly, smiling middle managers greeted him at the airport. He told them that he was on a tight schedule and that he would like to arrange an appointment the next day with the company executives. "Yes, Yes," the managers said as he was whisked to his hotel. At this point in the story the more experienced "China hands" sitting around the table would nod and chuckle knowing the executive had already made three mistakes. The next day the executive was picked up at the hotel by the welcoming committee and whisked off to tour the company's manufacturing facilities. Throughout the day, the executive kept asking when he could meet with the senior manager to start negotiations. They assured him that the meeting would occur shortly and meantime there were other

The absolute proof of a successful contract comes when the check clears the bank.

■■■ INTELLECTUAL PROPERTY RIGHTS

As a Western entrepreneur doing business in China the most likely crime you'll encounter is theft—of your intellectual property. In addition to cyber espio-

places to visit. Exhausted, the executive returned to his room still without having started negotiations or even meeting the senior managers.

On the third and final day of his stay, the executive was now in a panic. He only had a few hours left to negotiate a contract before his return flight. After desperate pleading with his welcoming committee, they finally assured him the senior manager would see him before he left. The welcoming committee picked up the executive to drive him to the airport and on the way, they also picked up the senior manager! With only minutes left to negotiate, the executive signed a contract that was highly unfavorable to his company.

So what were the three mistakes the executive made? The first mistake was to start discussing business right away; the second, believing that only one person in a Chinese company is in charge of making decisions; and the third, expecting quick results.

nage, IP theft takes place through bribed employees, on-site theft, and reverse-engineering.

Although China is signatory to various international copyright, patent, and intellectual property rights agreements, enforcement is another story. A recent report estimates that China is responsible for some 70% of the $300 billion each year the U.S. loses due to the theft of intellectual property.

True Stories: Vegas Pays a Visit to Taipei

Nothing travels faster than gossip among the expat communities. One of the hot topics in Taiwan several years ago was the story of two very big and brawny "Private Investigators" looking for an American businessman stationed in Taipei. The businessman didn't show up for work that week and his whereabouts were unknown. The plot thickened when it was discovered that the investigators were working for a Las Vegas casino. Several days later, accompanied by local police, the investigators closed down a local plastic injection molding company and confiscated all their equipment. The story finally broke in the expat newsletter gossip column. Someone had reverse-engineered several denominations of poker chips from an undisclosed casino complete with embedded RFID chip and was having them manufactured in bulk and shipped to Nevada to be laundered back through the casinos. The operation was said to have netted millions. The factory owner was not charged with any crime, though his equipment remained impounded. The American businessman thought to be behind it all was never seen or heard from again.

There are several ways of to protect your intellectual property in China, though none are foolproof. The first is to register your IP with the appropriate Chinese bureaus. Your North American patent or trademark may not be recognized by the Chinese government, so having Chinese registrations will add weight to any court filings you may make in the future.

Presumably, whatever product you are making, or having made, is labor intensive and has multiple components. Consider having different companies manufacture the components separately and then another company assemble the final product. In this way no one factory see the entire process, thus making it harder to re-create the end product and impossible to simply add a midnight shift to produce your product for the black market.

To protect digital property rights you will need encryption schemes, although thus far the Digital Rights Management systems tried in the past have largely failed to prevent piracy.

You are more likely to have your ideas stolen in a joint-venture agreement than if you set up the manufacturing in China yourself. A rule of thumb: if your product is hot with a huge market demand, it will likely be pirated.

Business
Entertainment

Speak deferentially, listen respectfully, follow his commands, and accord with him in everything. He will never imagine you might be in conflict with him. Our treacherous measures will then be settled.

The Six Secret Teachings of the Tai Gong

■■■ DINNER GUEST

Taking a visiting business associate out to dinner is a universal practice and especially popular in China. Since the Chinese prefer to establish social connections with the people they do business with, the dinner party is the premier venue in which to accomplish this. Naturally, you should be aware of several cultural niceties.

Business dinners, or more accurately banquets, are the norm, although business lunches are growing in popularity. Business breakfasts are almost unheard of.*

Dinners usually begin around 6:30 or 7:00 and last for 2 hours or more. If you are a guest, you should arrive on time. If you arrive about 15 minutes early to a banquet your Chinese hosts and counterparts will probably be present before the proceedings officially begin, and this may give you time for some introductions and small talk.

Banquets are usually held at restaurants that cater to dinner banquets, of which there are many, and your dinner may be hosted at a large table, a private room, or even an entire floor of the restaurant.

Wait for a host or hostess to seat you. In Chinese culture there is a seating etiquette based on hierarchy. According to tradition, the seat in the middle of the table, facing the door, is reserved for the guest of honor, who sits opposite the host. If there is no guest of honor, the most senior member sits in the center seat. The next most honored guest will be seated to the left of the guest of honor. If the host has any doubts about the correct order of precedence for his guests, he will seat them based on age.†

---

* Except in Guangdong, Hangzhou, and Fujian provinces where "Morning Tea" is very popular.

† This is not consistent throughout China. In Shandong banquet culture, for example, the reverse is true, with the host seated furthest from the door and the seat of honor to the host's right.

■■■ TABLE MANNERS

The easiest way to learn proper table etiquette is simply to follow the host. Tradition requires the host be the first to begin eating and drinking. As soon as the host has begun eating, the rest of the party can proceed with the meal.

Those new to Chinese banquets are often surprised to find that as many as twenty or more courses are served. The mistake is to eat too much from the first several courses and then have to refuse the last courses, which may appear rude. Conversely, filling your bowl over the brim is also considered inappropriate. You can ask your host how many dishes are to be served and pace yourself by lightly sampling each dish. Often the restaurant will have a written menu on the table listing each course. Make some small talk by inquiring about the history and significance of certain dishes; you'll be able to tell how many more courses are still to come.

While in many Western countries cleaning your plate is a sign of appreciation, cleaning your plate in China can be seen as an insult since it implies that you were not given enough food and had to scrape every last morsel from your plate or bowl. To avoid such an embarrassment, the host will order more food than the number of guests attending can eat, since he or she loses face if there are not leftovers at the end of a meal.

By the end of the dinner you should leave some food on your plate; leaving a dish untouched may also give offense suggesting you are not satisfied with the flavor. For the sake of politeness, you should try a small portion of each dish.

Contrary to popular perception, rice is seldom served as one of the main courses. It is considered by many Chinese to be filler along the lines of a dinner roll and is usually not served until near the end of a meal. If you want to eat rice with your meal, it is perfectly acceptable to ask the server to bring you the rice early.

Dishes such as clams and shellfish that you eat with your hands will be accompanied by a second cup of tea or hot water that is used to dip and clean your fingers in.

During a meal, complimenting the host on the quality and taste of the food you are eating is welcomed and an expected topic of conversation.

Unlike Western tradition, soup is served near the end of the meal to "fill in the cracks."

Dessert is never a major part of the meal. Restaurants that are more modern will include some sweet cakes (although what is sweet according to Chinese tastes is seldom as sweet as what Western palates expect). The meal has reached a definite conclusion when fruit is served and hot towels are presented.

It would be rude of the host or hostess to initiate the guests' departure. If you are with other Chinese guests, follow their cue when to leave. If you are on your own, then leave shortly after the meal is finished. Unlike in the West where it is considered impolite to "eat and run," in China everyone leaves soon after the meal is finished.

Tipping is generally considered an insult in China. It is sometimes expected, however, in some of the bigger hotels and by younger service personnel. When in doubt, discreetly ask your companions or the host what the protocol is for that establishment.

To attract the attention of servers do not raise or point your finger. The accepted hand signal is to turn your palm down, waving your fingers toward yourself.

Generally, the host will bid good evening to everyone at the door and stay behind to settle the bill with the restaurant.

■■■ SPITTING AND SMOKING

Some dinner manners that are acceptable in China are contrary to Western manners and may make you feel uncomfortable. These include: slurping your soup or noodles, burping, reaching in front of others for dishes and other items, and tossing your discarded bones, gristle, fish skin, clam shells, peanut shells, or other discarded food right on the tablecloth next to your plate, and, in some restaurants, even on the floor. Most big-city restaurants now provide an extra bowl or dish to use instead of the tablecloth.

Even more offensive to Western sensibilities is the common practice of clearing one's throat and spitting the discharge on the floor or out of the window. Everyone does it, more frequently during winter months when many people have colds and runny noses. Try not to let it bother you and do not look disgusted. Just remember to touch as few public surfaces as possible and wash your hands to the point of compulsion.

Thankfully, breaking wind in public is definitely impolite.

Smoking is very popular in China; many Chinese smoke more than a pack a day. Non-smoking areas are practically unheard of, and although the Chinese government has begun paying lip service to public health concerns about smoking, there is little indication that this is taken seriously. Since tax revenues from tobacco sales are a major source of income for the government, nonsmoking campaigns are likely to be unsuccessful.

The Chinese will be offended if you tell them not to smoke; however, it is fine to refuse a cigarette politely if one is offered to you. As with drinking hard liquor, smoking in public is largely a male activity.

Another common complaint of Westerners is that the Chinese do not practice common courtesy to strangers in public places, especially in forming orderly lines and waiting one's turn. Do not be offended if you are pushed and shoved when standing in a line. In public, everyone is a stranger, so Confucian etiquette does not apply. Also, be warned that the Chinese "personal space," or comfort zone, is closer in public than most Westerners are accustomed to.

■■■ TEA DRINKING

The Chinese have been cultivating tea for over 5,000 years, and an important part of Chinese entertaining is the tea-drinking ritual. Tea is used as a medicine, a tonic, a social stimulant, even a way of life. Like fine wine, certain brands of tea can fetch up to US$200 per ounce or more. Tea is served before a meeting or during meals to establish social goodwill similar to the West's tradition of "breaking bread."

Serving tea in China involves some ritual activities but is not nearly as formal as the fabled Japanese tea ceremony. In China, everyone simply takes turns pouring tiny cups of tea for each other. When drinking the tea you should sit straight, with your right

Curious Fact: Finger Tapping

When someone is pouring tea, you will often see the recipient tap the table with three fingers three times. This is a polite form of saying thank you and has its origin in an incident from Chinese history.

Legend says that during the Qing dynasty an emperor wanted to see how the common people really lived and decided to inspect his lands by going incognito and pretending to be an ordinary traveler. While visiting South China, he once went into a teahouse with his companions and in order not to arouse suspicion as to his special status, took his turn pouring tea for his courtiers.

His shocked companions wanted to *kowtow* (ritual bow) to him for the great honor he was doing them, but this would reveal his identity. Therefore, the emperor told them to discreetly tap three fingers on the table. One finger represented the bowed head and the other two the prostrate arms. This is the origin for the custom of discreetly "tapping your thanks" whenever someone pours you a cup of tea. Likewise, when you offer a light for someone's cigarette they may tap the back of your wrist, also signifying thanks.

hand holding the cup and the fingers of your left hand lightly touching the bottom of the cup as you drink.

Throughout the dinner your teacup will be continually refilled by servers or other hosts. If you do not want a refill of tea, leave your cup half full.

The polite way to ask for the teapot to be refilled with fresh hot water is is to lift the lid off and let it hang loose by the wire or cord that binds it to the pot, or balanced on the handle.

■■■ CHOPSTICKS

As a Westerner, you may request to use a fork or spoon without causing any insult. However, making an effort to use chopsticks shows a willingness to learn Chinese culture. Even if you give up in frustration, you will have earned points for trying.

Chopsticks seem ungainly to the first-time user but with a little practice, you can become adept quickly. Chinese cooking techniques ensure that most items are precut so you never need a knife to cut your food. The chopsticks are used like tongs to pick food up.

When eating rice, hold the bowl in your left hand close to your mouth and use the chopsticks in your right hand to shovel the rice into your mouth. It may seem uncouth to shovel food directly from a dish into your mouth, but it is the only practical method of eating rice when using chopsticks.

Noodles can be cut using the chopsticks like scissors, which takes some skill, but it is more common to just scoop some into your mouth and slurp them in.

Traditionally the dishes are placed in the center

How to Use Chopsticks

1. Hold one stick in the webbing between thumb and forefinger and index finger.

2. Hold the second stick as you would a pencil alongside your forefinger.

3. The first stick remains stationary while the second stick is moved up and down.

---

of the table, usually on a Lazy Susan, and everyone uses their own chopsticks to transfer food from the communal plates to their own bowls or plates. However, to stop the spread of such communicable diseases as tuberculosis, serving spoons or larger chopsticks may accompany each dish, and you should use these rather than your own chopsticks to take a portion of food.

When you are finished eating, place your chopsticks on the table or on a chopstick rest, a brass or porcelain paperweight-like object. Do not lay your chopsticks parallel on top of your bowl; it is bad luck. Sticking your chopsticks straight up in your rice bowl is also unlucky because in this position they resemble the incense sticks used in Chinese funeral rituals.

Toothpicks are usually offered between courses and at the conclusion of a meal. When using a toothpick, use your free hand to cover your mouth as you do when you cough. Toothpicks are also useful and socially acceptable for picking up those slippery meal items such as button mushrooms and Jell-O cubes.

■■■ DIM SUM RESTAURANTS

If you are in southern China, you will likely be taken to a dim sum restaurant. *Dim sum* is a Cantonese term that refers to a brunch or light lunch eaten sometime between morning and early afternoon. In Mandarin, it is called *dian xin*, meaning "to touch the heart" or "to order to one's heart's content," since dim sum consists of a wide selection of snacks with combinations of meat, vegetables, seafood, and fruit. The larger specialist dim sum restaurants will prepare hundreds of such dishes, as well as augment the small dishes with larger platters of fried rice or noodles. Each small dish is served in a bamboo or stainless-steel steamer or on a small plate. The dishes are brought to your table stacked like hatboxes one on top of the other, or are pushed around on little carts wheeled about the restaurant by servers. Dim sum is also called *yum cha* in the Cantonese dialect, which literally means "to drink tea" but refers to the same type of dining experience.

Curious Facts: Fish Flipping

Most banquets will include a fried or steamed whole fish dish. You are supposed to peel off portions of the meat from the bone until the upper half of the fish is picked clean. The host or server will then use another pair of chopsticks to remove the fish skeleton so the lower half can be accessed. Why not just turn the fish over? The reason is an ancient superstition whose origins lie with South China's fishing families. Flipping the fish over could result in bad luck and cause the fishing boat that caught your fish to capsize.

Dim sum restaurants are typically crowded, noisy, and hectic, and unless you or your host is a VIP, it is everyone for themselves. You will first need to grab any vacant chairs available, and you should not be shy about summoning all the dim sum cart ladies, done by waving your hand, palm downward, as they wheel around the room. While generally the servers follow a set path, it is not uncommon for people to get up and take an item from a cart. The reason behind this is: if you wait too long, chances are someone else is going to come along and grab all the good dishes before they get to you. The process is somewhat akin to a baseball game where hot dog or popcorn vendors walk around the stands carrying their trays, and it is up to those in the seats to call out and attract attention to get service. You need to call every cart to your table since each may carry different dishes.

As the cart pulls up to your table you can ask what dishes are in the bamboo baskets or covered dishes, or if no one at your table can speak Chinese, you can just lift up the lids of the baskets and dishes to see what is in them.

The emptied baskets and plates are used as "counters" by your table waiter to calculate your final bill. Keep them on the table and never try to place an empty basket back on a trolley, since you may be accused of trying to duck the bill.

Another method used to keep track of what you ordered is a small card placed on your table that the servers will stamp with a small, numbered chop each time you choose a basket or plate of dim sum.

A polite way to let the waiter know that you have finished is to lay your chopsticks across each other on your bowl or plate. If the waiter is too busy to notice simply resort to the hand-waving gesture again.

A steaming pot of tea is served as soon as you sit down to dim sum. Drinking tea here is not as formal as at banquets. Do not be alarmed if you see fellow diners using the tea to first wash and heat their cups and then pour the waste into the nearest empty container.

■■■ CONVERSATION TOPICS

A single conversation across the table with a wise man is better than ten years mere study of books.
Chinese Proverb

Unlike Western custom, business in China is not discussed during the meal. This is the time to create social, not business connections.

Chinese will often ask questions considered a little too personal in the West, such as your age, income, and marital status. If you do not want to reveal this information, remain polite and give an unspecific answer. Remember that negative replies are considered impolite. Do not express irritation with the questioner, since this will cause him or her loss of face.

In older Chinese culture, the equivalent to asking "How are you?" is, literally, "Have you eaten?" This questions harkens back to agrarian times when floods and droughts often brought famines. The exchange is a formality and does not require you to recount your lunch menu. Simply answer, "Yes," even if you have not actually eaten.

Try to learn and use at least a few words in Mandarin. Chinese are especially appreciative toward foreigners speaking their language, and your efforts will go a long way toward establishing mutual trust.

Do not be surprised or worried if there are periods of silence during your business or dinner conversations. It is a sign of politeness and of thought. Do not be quick to fill the silence with words, as it will make you appear impatient and immature. Also, be careful not to interrupt during a conversation.

Chinese tend to evaluate a person in accordance with that person's relationship within a family, so talking about your and your host's families is a welcome topic of conversation. Small talk is especially important at the beginning of a meeting.

Welcome Topics
Chinese scenery, landmarks.
Weather, climate, and geography in China.
Your travels in other countries.
Your positive experiences traveling in China.
Chinese art and history.

Topics to Avoid
Naturally, politics should not be discussed. If on the mainland, avoid mentioning Taiwan if possible. If the subject comes up, never refer to Taiwan as "The Republic of China" or "Nationalist China." The correct term is "Taiwan Province," or just "Taiwan." Also, refrain from using the terms such as "Red China" or "Communist China."

Finally, beware of praising the Japanese or to be seen as being especially good friends with them. Nor should you praise Shanghai in front of natives of Beijing or Hong Kong, and vice versa.

Because the Chinese language is so complex, a lot of Chinese humor is based on the use of puns and can be very sophisticated. Avoid the temptation to tell crude jokes along the lines of "A guy walks into a bar . . ." The Chinese sense of humor is quite a bit different from the West's, and most jokes do not translate well into Chinese. The best that can happen is you will have to explain the joke, and then you will make everyone lose face because they did not understand and laugh at your attempt at humor.

Unlike the Western custom, compliments in China are not graciously accepted with a "thank you," but rather with a self-deprecating "not at all" or "it was nothing." Do not be overly flattering. If you can speak a few words of Chinese, someone might try to compliment you. Do not say thank you, but rather, *bu gandang* (I'm not worthy of such a compliment). Your modesty will be even more impressive than your ability to speak the language. Chinese look upon accepting and acknowledging direct praise as being smarmy and in poor taste.

■■■ DRINKING

Let us get drunk today, while we have wine; the
sorrows of tomorrow may be borne tomorrow.
                                        Chinese Proverb

An important facet of forming personal relationships with your Chinese counterparts is to earn their
respect and trust. You can earn bonus points if you
participate in the tradition of drinking and toasting games that take place during or after many business dinners. Drinking alcohol is a way for people to
drop their guard, and refusing to participate may be
regarded with suspicion, since it implies that you have
something to hide. It is often through such drinking
rituals that classic male bonding occurs and business
deals are cemented. Although women can take part by
having a sip or two, a woman who can drink her male
counterpart under the table will not win respect the
way another male would.

Toasting is usually done with beer served in small
glasses, and it is the host of a banquet that offers the
first toast. It is always a good idea for the guest to
return the toast either right away or after a few courses
have been served. Do not pour your own drink as it
shows a lack of protocol.

The Chinese will understand if you are unable

to drink alcohol. If you prefer not to drink alcohol, it is perfectly acceptable to toast with a soft drink, glass of juice, or mineral water. Another face-saving way of bowing out is stating that you have medical reasons for not drinking.

If you are the guest of honor, you may find yourself on the receiving end of everyone else's personal toast. This is both a form of courtesy and a test of the Westerner's renowned propensity to hold his liquor (women are exempted from having to demonstrate this ability).

Typically, each Chinese host will raise his or her glass to you and say the traditional toast, *ganbei* ("bottoms up!"). You should likewise raise your glass, say *ganbei* (pronounced gone bay: it literally means "to clean the glass"), and down the entire glass. Since this is a personal toast, only you and the dinner guest who proposed the toast are expected to drink. Then the next Chinese guest will propose a personal toast. If you are sitting with, say, twelve Chinese guests, you can expect to down twelve 2-ounce glasses of beer for every one they consume.

Fortunately, most Chinese are not big drinkers and two rounds of toasts are usually enough to make everyone feel a little light-headed. Occasionally someone will up the ante and start toasting with a potent clear alcohol, typically 160 proof (80% alco-

Curious Facts: Origins of Karaoke Prostitutes

Many of China's karaoke clubs act as fronts for prostitution, a variation of the hostess-style clubs where gentlemen pay for the drinks of attractive young women who will entertain with a song. These women may or may not also provide sexual services; they are in the higher level of the trade, which means they choose which clients to accept and derive most of their income through a commission on drink sales and tips. Many of the women who work karaoke clubs are there to find positions as a "Little Wife," which is a long-term exclusive contract with a single patron—a formal mistress.

The tradition of singing prostitutes goes back at least as far as the Han dynasty (206 BCE–CE 220), when emperors

hol), that tastes like jet fuel. If you have the stomach and liver for it, downing a glass of this brew will establish your machismo.

Once you have had enough of drinking games, you can bow out and save face by saying you cannot drink any more liquor but you would like to offer one last toast wishing everyone good fortune.

Another common phrase used during banquets and dinners is *suiyi* (sway yee), which translates roughly as "make yourself at home." If someone is toasting you and saying *suiyi* it implies that you do not have to drain your glass but rather may sip as much as

are recorded as hiring women to entertain the troops in the field much like a USO show. In more recent times, some girls were trained from childhood to entertain wealthy male clients through singing and dancing in special meeting houses. Although many provided sexual services not all did and instead lived off the sponsorship of one or more wealthy male clients. The hope of many was to end up marrying their sponsor and leaving the trade behind for a new life.

A similar tradition was adopted by the Japanese sometime during Japan's Heian period (794–1185). Most Westerners are more familiar with this Japanese version: the Geisha.

you please. Conversely, if you wish to toast someone and you do not wish to drain your glass again you can do so by repeating this phrase.

Also, bear in mind that a table full of people at a Chinese banquet will usually all drink the same thing. Do not expect a server to take orders for several different kinds of beer and liquor (although at the larger hotels, a wider selection of beverages may be available).

At a formal meal, do not sit down and begin sipping your drink by yourself. Instead, you must toast or be toasted in order to sip.

■■■ KARAOKE

Throughout history, music and singing have been an important part of dining and entertaining across East Asia. Before the electronic age, large restaurants would hire singers to entertain, while poorer classes would simply sing among themselves. The sudden, widespread popularity of karaoke in recent decades occurred mainly because it allowed everyone, rich or poor, to sing as if they were the star of the show and to thus take turns sharing the spotlight. In China, it is almost standard practice to take guests out to a kara-oke club after dinner. If you wish to establish close relations with Chinese, going to karaoke is one of the best ways of doing it.

Most karaoke clubs have Chinese, Japanese, and English songs. Be prepared to sing at least one song. The good news is that foreign guests need not put on a great performance, and any attempt to sing will be greeted with much praise and applause.

It is customary for the host for the night to pick up all bills, including all entertainment, and it is impo-lite to fight for the bill or worse, split the bill.

While karaoke is a popular activity, some Chinese may regard it as somewhat low-class, so you should not bring up the subject unless you are invited to go.

■■■ FAMILY VISITING

Home entertaining is very popular in China. If you are invited to a Chinese home, arrive on time, but not too early. It is customary to remove your shoes before entering the main living quarters.

Chinese etiquette requires that you bring a small gift as well. Flowers, fruits, or a box of cookies or biscuits are standard presents. A bottle of liquor is usually welcome, but be sure to check beforehand whether the recipient drinks alcohol. During meals, it is customary for the host to ask you to have more food or alcohol. Remember, cleaning your plate is considered an insult, so to avoid disappointing your hosts accept a second helping and leave some on the plate afterward.

Generally, the same dining etiquette applies to home diners as well as to restaurant banquets. The household's eldest female will be in charge of cooking and will typically prepare many dishes. Compliments on the food are greatly appreciated and expected.

■■■ DINNER HOST

If a man does not receive guests at home, he will meet with very few hosts abroad.

Chinese Proverb

If you have been the guest of honor at one or more banquets, proper etiquette requires you to reciprocate by hosting a banquet. The Chinese expect a boss to be a leader both inside and outside the organization by taking a leadership role in social entertaining as well.

Be sure to rely on the advice of your Chinese partners or interpreters to choose an appropriate time and place to ensure you do not host on an unlucky day or national holiday.

The reciprocal banquet should be of similar value but should never surpass your hosts' by being more lavish or expensive. This implies that your hosts were being stingy and will cause them to lose face.

Most Chinese are unfamiliar with foreign foods and are reluctant to experiment when it comes to their diet, and most will probably not like Western food. The safest course is to take your guests to a good Chinese restaurant. Many restaurants cater to just such business banquets.

If you are hosting a banquet, you should arrive at least 30 minutes before your guests.

According to tradition, the seat in the middle of the table, facing the door, is reserved for the guest of honor, who sits opposite the host. The next most honored guest will be seated to the left of the guest of honor. Follow this seating pattern if you are hosting a banquet or a meal in your residence, whether for business or social reasons.

When inviting people to your home, avoid serving dairy products such as cheese; many Chinese are lactose intolerant.

Remember that as the host it is your job to propose the first toast, start the meal, and then end the meal no more than 30 minutes after the last dish has been served.

■■■ HOSTESS CLUBS

Present him with licentious musicians and dancers to change his customs. Or give him beautiful women to bewilder him.

Chia Lin

Notorious in Hong Kong and Taiwan, and recently resurrected on the mainland, are the hostess clubs. These are opulent nightclubs staffed by attractive women who cater to businessmen there to close and celebrate deals. Most clubs are exclusively Chinese while some clubs cater to foreign businessmen. The women are typically called "hostesses," and men pay for their company either on a minute-by-minute rate or by buying them exorbitantly priced drinks. Some hostesses are also available for sexual services, either on the premises or off. Credit cards are accepted, and a discreet receipt is provided under the businesslike heading of an international trading or consulting services company so that corporate accounting departments, or taxpayers, back home will be none the wiser.

A common myth is that sly Chinese businessmen bring their foreign clients to such establishments where, besotted and bedazzled, the victim gladly signs away his profit margin on cutthroat contracts. However, as we learned earlier, business is rarely conducted during social events. Being invited to attend a hostess club as guest of your Chinese business associates is rare and occurs only after you have already had a long business history together. The occasional exceptions include visiting government representatives. It is more common for local businessmen to entertain Chinese officials, which is seen as bribery, and special laws have been passed that focus on prosecuting such forms of bureaucratic corruption.

The usual dining and drinking etiquette applies when in a hostess club. Should you be the type who likes to gamble his or her* career on a night's dalliance, be sure to check whether a particular hostess even offers such a service and if so whether she will agree.

* Japan has "host" clubs where the sex roles are reversed, and this trend may find its way to China shortly.

The hostesses are allowed to choose and decline offers based on their own feelings at the time. If the hostess agrees then you would first have to "buy her out" of the club. This is, in theory, to compensate the club owner for the loss of business the hostess would have provided selling drinks. Club owners are thereby theoretically absolved of the crimes of pandering or running a brothel. The buy-out fees are quite hefty and only allow you to leave the premises with the hostess in tow. Any services in addition to the buy-out fee must be negotiated with the hostess. An expensive dinner, drinks, and even a little shopping beforehand is also often expected from Western high rollers.

Business
Gift-Giving

*Assist him (the enemy) in his licentiousness and
indulgence in music in order to dissipate his will.
Make him generous gifts of pearls, and jade, and
ply him with beautiful women.*

The Six Secret Teachings of the Tai Gong

Official policy in Chinese business culture forbids
giving gifts, as this may be considered bribery, which
is illegal. However, gift-giving, as indeed bribery, has
long been a part of business culture both in China and
in the West. Choosing the correct type of gifts and
knowing the correct way to present those gifts can
make the difference between a successful venture and
criminal charges.

An old Chinese aphorism says "courtesy demands
reciprocity." This means that should you give a gift,

you are also obligating the recipient to give you a gift in return. Differences between Western and Chinese wages is such that should you give a gift that is too expensive, you are obliging that person to reciprocate with an equally expensive gift, which may place a financial strain on your host.

The best choice is a gift that expresses some unique aspect of your country or company, such as handicrafts or an illustrated book. Bring a supply of these items with you so you will be prepared to reciprocate should you be presented with unexpected gifts later in your itinerary.

Giving a modest gift to the entire company or management team, rather than to an individual, is perfectly acceptable provided you specify that the gift is from the company you represent. In this case, the gift is presented to the leader of the Chinese management team, who will accept it on behalf of the entire team.

If you wish to give a gift to an individual, you must do it privately, in the context of friendship, not business. Giving a gift in the presence of other people will only cause embarrassment, and possibly create problems for the recipient, given both the strict rules against bribery and the affront of rewarding a single individual instead of the whole team.

Chinese etiquette requires that a person decline a gift three times before finally accepting so as not to appear covetous. You will have to be insistent until they accept. Deprecate the gift by explaining it is a mere token of appreciation for your treatment as a guest. Once they accept the gift, express gratitude. If the recipient did not open your gift, this does not mean that he or she is not interested in it. It is polite to open a gift after you leave.

Should you be given a gift, which is highly likely, you will likewise be expected to refuse three times before giving in. You should protest the expense the host has gone through.

As with business cards, the proper way to both give and receive gifts is with both hands. Finally, do not make too much of a fuss over the gift; just accept it with a sincere thank you.

■■■ GOOD GIFT IDEAS

A good cognac or other fine liqueur, preferably pack-aged in the decorative display box that you can buy at the duty-free store, is always a safe bet. A fine pen (but not with red ink, of course), small solar calculators, or electronic gadgets are all modest but appreciated gifts.

Gifts of food are acceptable, but not at dinner parties or other occasions where appetizers and meals will be served. Candy and fruit baskets, however, are acceptable thank-you gifts to send after these events.

True Stories: The Green Hat

A senior foreign executive thought to promote his company by handing out baseball caps with the company's logo on them as gifts. In order to show the company's commitment to a clean environment, green was the color chosen for the hats. No one put on the hats since, unbeknownst to the confused executive, "wearing a green hat" was a Chinese euphemism for being a cuckold.[9]

Since the number 8 is considered one of the luckiest numbers in Chinese culture, giving or receiving eight of any item, such as eight fruits, is seen as a gesture of goodwill.

■■■ BAD GIFT IDEAS

Scissors, knives, or other sharp objects represent the severing of a friendship or other bonds. Straw sandals, clocks, handkerchiefs, and anything white, blue, or black are all associated with funerals and are therefore very unlucky. Never give four of any item.

As with all things Chinese, there is even symbolism in gift-wrapping. Red is always a "lucky" color for gift-wrap. If you insist on breaking with tradition, stick to festive colors and avoid black or white for reasons previously mentioned. Don't wrap a gift before arriving in China, as it may be unwrapped in customs.

■■■ BRIBES

In the days of the old Tai-Pans, the polite term for bribery was "fragrant grease" (*xiang you*). Bribe money was the "grease" needed to get the machinery of government and business rolling. While the Chinese government and corporate culture work hard to promote honest and legal practices, you may nevertheless come across situations where bribery is either hinted at or demanded. What should you do? Play along and make the deal, or take a stand but risk losing out to a competitor without a similar commitment to honesty?

The answer is simple, since as a foreigner it is almost impossible to play this game without it turning into a disaster. The consequences in terms of capital losses, potential criminal charges, and loss of corporate reputation would be greater than any advantage. The only position a foreign business person should take is that of the professional and honest broker of goods and information.

However, your Chinese agents, partners, or intermediaries may have their own methods of greasing the wheels, which you will likely never know about, and being overly inquisitive about the details of how they got things done might not be appreciated.

First, you need to establish a clear moral position.

When initially presenting your company's credentials to a Chinese company or government bureau,

True Stories: The Golden Teacup

A senior manager at a four-star, but otherwise unremarkable, hotel in China proudly displayed the winning notification on the employee's bulletin board. The glossy full-color brochure announced that the hotel had just won the International Golden Teacup Award for outstanding service and cuisine as decided by an international panel of experts. The senior manager was personally invited to attend the gala awards ceremony and received an all-expenses-paid trip to Spain for a week.

The International Golden Teacup Award was sponsored by a large hotel supply company that had recently been awarded a contract signed by the senior manager of the very hotel that had just won the Golden Teacup Award. Two blocks away, another hotel also won the Golden Teacup Award, and its manager was off to Spain for a week as well. Not surprisingly, he had also recently signed a contract with the same hotel supply company.

make a special point of emphasizing that your company is also renowned for its high ethical and professional standards. When the time is right, explain that everyone on your management team has signed legal documents prohibiting him or her from receiving any monetary compensation from any negotiation. Present this as though you are trying to assure your Chinese counterparts that they will be treated in the most open and honest manner. The message it

Curious Facts: Red Envelopes

When it comes to formal gift-giving occasions such as weddings, birthdays, and New Year's, the Chinese have a pragmatic approach. Instead of gifts, they simply give cash. Gifts of cash are always placed in a red envelope or *hong bao*. The red color of the packet symbolizes good luck, and the amount of money in the packet is often some lucky number (see the discussion on page 86). In the past, *hong bao* was also a euphemism for bribing officials.

really sends is that, by not being susceptible to receiving bribes, you would naturally not be expected to pay them either.

Before entering negotiations, be sure to learn as much as possible about the Chinese company or agency you are going to be dealing with, including personal details about the managers and executives you will be meeting.

Depending on the scale of the deal, it may be wise to invest in the services of an investigative agency to do a background check into the organization. Such a check will help you avoid the many "paper tigers": companies that have an impressive façade but are instead empty fronts used to extract bribes and assorted ill gains.

If you are going to do business in China through an agent, take special care to ensure that the agent is not one of many that rely primarily on bribes in dealing with bureaucracy and suppliers.

Should your shining reputation fail to discourage such activities and you are asked for a bribe, do not show anger. Apologize sincerely and explain that if you agree to any kind of unauthorized payment you will be fired and may face criminal charges in your home country when you return.

Instead of paying the bribe there are alternatives you can offer. These involve giving your counterpart "face." Instead of exchanging cash or gifts, which would constitute hard evidence and could land everyone in jail, you could offer to award your counterpart the title "Manager of the Year," for which he or she will be honored at a large banquet and presented with a brass plaque. By giving someone face, you improve that person's political leverage within his or her business or political circles, and that leverage can be used to advantage in other deals.

If you are really backed into a corner, you can always agree to try to arrange some kind of authorized consideration, such as a consultant's fee, but you will need to submit certain paperwork first. This will buy you a couple of days until you can consult with your legal department on what the best course of action might be.

Shopping

Though a poor man should live in the midst of a noisy market, no one will ask about him; though a rich man should bury himself among the mountains, his relations will come to him from a distance.

Chinese Proverb

If this is your first time in China, you will at some point have to go shopping in order to bring back the obligatory souvenirs for friends and family. This can be a hair-pulling ordeal—trying to negotiate the throngs, the pushy salespeople, the exchange rates, and language barrier—but the payoff is some great bargains on quality goods. Shopping is also a great way to practice your negotiating skills.

When you buy something from a street vendor at a night market, or from a small shop, haggling over price is the norm. Often you will find that items will not have a price tag. If you have to ask the price, then know that you are going to have to bargain. Even if there is a price tag, it does not mean you cannot bargain, so you should always try to get a lower price.

In most Western-style department stores or the old reliable Friendship Stores, you do not normally bargain; however, if you are going to purchase multiple items of a single gift or are purchasing something quite expensive, then by all means try to negotiate a better price.[10] If they give you an immediate no or do not offer to lower their price, then stop trying to haggle any further.

As a rule of thumb, a vendor's opening price is usually double the price what they are willing to accept. Start your counteroffer at about 30% of the asking price and haggle back and forth until you arrive near the middle.

Never, however, haggle the shopkeeper down, agree on a price, and then not buy the item. You can offer a lower amount than the asking price and see if the shopkeeper or clerk comes down on price. But if you agree to that price and then walk away you will have insulted the vendor and shown poor etiquette.

Most salespeople are helpful and polite. Sometimes they may be too helpful and follow you around while you browse, which can be annoying at times. Learn the simple phrase "I'm just looking" (*Wo jiu kan*

kan yi xia) and they will usually back off and wait for you to call them over.

Sometimes you will see Chinese shoppers arguing or haggling loudly with vendors especially at night markets. If you come across a vendor with a confrontational attitude, do not take it personally; this is just business. Keeping a calm exterior works best, although as a foreigner you do not need to raise your voice, nor would it look appropriate for you to do so.

Polite and friendly is definitely the way to go. Always smile, stay calm, and do not show anger or frustration. A shopkeeper may assume a friendly person is less likely to haggle and will just politely offer a lower counteroffer and smile. When the vendor no longer gives you a counteroffer, say thank you and start to walk away. If they stop you at the door or chase you outside, you know they are ready to make their lowest offer.

■■■ SHOPPING TIPS

Most vendors have a pocket calculator that they will use to punch in their asking price to show it to you. You can clear their input and input your counteroffer, and so on until a price has been agreed upon. As a fail-safe you can also bring a medium felt marker and a notebook so that you can write down the price of your offer and counteroffers. Most Chinese understand the decimal notation for writing numbers and can write down their asking price and counteroffers on your pad, which will help overcome the language barrier.

Another method used by the Chinese for counting and especially for bargaining is a series of gestures that indicate the numbers from 1 to 10 using the fingers of one hand. It is thought that this method was developed in earlier times by merchants who negotiated prices by inserting their hands into each other's sleeves and using hand signals to indicate offers and counteroffers. Since this was all done out of view of potential competitors, other clients would not know what the previous customer paid.

It is an easy system to learn, and using it when bargaining will impress your Chinese counterparts. The illustration on the following page shows the most common method.

An alternative for the number 10 uses both hands, with the index fingers perpendicularly crossed in an "X" and the palms facing in opposite directions.

In Taiwan and Hong Kong the signals for numbers 7, 8, and 9 are different in the following ways:

7: The thumb and index finger make an "L" as in the symbol for 8 (see illustration).

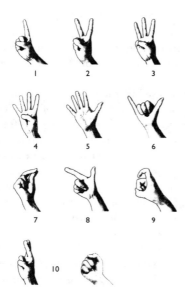

8: The thumb, index finger, and middle finger are extended.

9: Four digits excluding the little finger are extended. Since the little finger is not always independent of the ring finger, some might find this difficult to do.

■■■ USEFUL PHRASES WHEN SHOPPING

In China it is considered rude and disrespectful to say "I don't want" (*bu yao*). Instead, say *xie xie*, which in that context means "No, thank you." If the salesperson is too persistent then by all means say *bu yao*!

English	Pinyin	Pronunciation
How much?	duō shǎo qián?	dwo shao chee-yen
Too expensive	tài gui le	tie gway luh
Thank you	xiè xie	shee-yeh, shee-yeh
I am just looking.	wo zhǐ shì kàn kàn	wo jur shur kan kan
I don't want it	wǒ bù yào	waw boo yow
You are welcome	bù kè qì	boo kuh chee

Language

If there be no faith in our words, of what use are they?

Chinese Proverb

Mandarin is the main language of government, the media, and education in China and Taiwan, and one of the four official languages in Singapore. Originally the language spoken by Chinese officials, most of whom came from Beijing, Mandarin is known as *putonghua* (common language) in China, and *guoyu* (national language) in Taiwan.

Today the official romanization system used in China and in Western publications about China is *pinyin*. It is used for road signs, maps, brand names, computer input, Chinese Braille, telegrams, and many other purposes. It also appears in books for children and foreign students of Chinese. Pinyin uses all the letters of the Latin alphabet except *v*, but with often completely different pronunciations. It can take considerable time just to learn how to read and pronounce pinyin.

■■■ COMMON PHRASES IN MANDARIN

The following is a list of words and phrases that you may find useful. If you do not know how to pronounce pinyin do not worry; the approximate phonetic spelling of each word is also added. This will give you a start, and with a little help from Chinese associates, you will be able to learn and use a dozen phrases to good effect.

English	Pinyin	Pronunciation
Hello	ní hǎo	knee how
Good morning	zǎo	dzow
Goodnight	wǎn ān	wahn-ahn
Goodbye (see you later)	zài jiàn	dzai-jen
How are you?	ní hǎo ma?	knee how ma
Thank you	xiè xie	shee-yeah shee-yeah
You're welcome	bù kè qì	boo kuh chee
(May I ask?)	qǐng wèn	ching-wun
This	zhè gè	jeh-guh
That	nèi gè	neh-guh

English	Pinyin	Pronunciation
Excuse me/I'm sorry	duì bù qǐ	dooway boo chee
No problem	méi wèn tí	may wun tee
It doesn't matter	méi guān xi	may gwan she
Yes	shì de	shir duh
No	bù shi	boo shir
Good	hǎo	how
Wonderful	tài hǎo le	tie how luh
Do you speak English?	nǐ huì shuō yīng wén ma?	knee hway shwuh ying wen ma?
Do you understand?	nǐ dǒng ma?	knee dong muh?
I understand	wǒ dǒng	wuh dong
I don't understand	wǒ bù dǒng	wuh boo dong
What?	shén me?	shun muh?
What did you say?	nǐ shuō shén me	knee shwuh shun muh
What's your name?	nǐ jiào shén me míng zi?	knee jyow shun muh ming dzuh?
My name is Chris	wǒ de míng zi shì chris	wuh duh ming dzuh sher chris
I am tired	wǒ lèi le	wuh lay luh
hungry	wǒ è le	wuh uh luh
thirsty	wó kě le	wuh kuh luh
full	wó bǎo le	wuh bao luh

English	Pinyin	Pronunciation
That tastes good	hǎo chī	how chir
How much is it?	duō shǎo qián?	dwo shao chee-yen?
That's too expensive	tài guì le	tie gway luh
Please give me . . .	qíng gěi wǒ	ching gay wuh
I would like . . .	wǒ yào	wuh yao
Do you have . . .	yǒu méi yǒu	yoh may yoh
tea	chá	chah
water	shuǐ	shway
dumplings	jiǎo zi	ji-yow dzuh
rice	mǐ fàn	me fun
chicken	jī ròu	jee row
pork	zhū ròu	joo row
beef	niú ròu	knee-oh row
vegetables	shū cài	shoe ts-eye
Chinese currency	yuán	you-en
0	líng	ling
1	yī	yee
2	èr	are
3	sān	san
4	sì	ssuh
5	wǔ	woo
6	liù	leo
7	qī	chee
8	bā	bah

English	Pinyin	Pronunciation
9	jiǔ	ji-yeow
10	shí	sher
11	shí yī	sher-yee
12	shí èr	sher-R
20	èr shí	are-sher
21	èr shí yī	are-sher-yee
100	yī bǎi	yee bye

True Stories: Bite the Wax Tadpole

Something of an urban myth and an often-used example of the complexities of marketing in China is the story of the Coca-Cola Company's first efforts to market its product in China.

When Coca-Cola first entered the Chinese market in 1928, the company had no official representation of its name in Mandarin. Since Chinese is monosyllabic, they needed to find four Chinese characters whose pronunciations approximated the sounds "ko-ka-ko-la" without producing a nonsensical or adverse meaning when strung together as a written phrase. (Written Chinese employs about 40,000 different characters, of which about 200 are pronounced with sounds that could be used in forming the name "ko-ka-ko-la.")

While Coca-Cola was searching for a satisfactory combination of symbols to represent its name, Chinese

■■■ READING BODY LANGUAGE

> *A man's countenance is a sufficient index of his*
> *prosperity or adversity, without asking him any*
> *questions.*
>
> Chinese Proverb

Every good negotiator knows something about reading body language to gauge a client's attitudes and feelings. All cultures have somewhat differ-

shopkeepers created signs that combined characters whose pronunciations formed the string "ko-ka-ko-la," but they did so with no regard for the meanings of the written characters they used. The character for wax, pronounced "la," was used in many of these signs, resulting in strings that sounded like "ko-ka-ko-la" when pronounced but conveyed nonsensical meanings such as "female horse fastened with wax," "wax-flattened mare," or "bite the wax tadpole" when read.

Coca-Cola had to drop all characters that sounded like "la" because of their meanings and substituted them with one that was pronounced le ("luh"), meaning "joy." The final translation of the characters used means "to allow the mouth to be able to rejoice," which Coca-Cola registered as its Chinese trademark in 1928.

ent forms of nonverbal communication that may seem peculiar to Westerners, and the Chinese are no exception.

The first difference between Western and Eastern body language is personal space. The Chinese generally stand closer to each other than do Europeans and North Americans. Westerners, particularly Americans, find the Chinese stand a bit too close for their comfort, and will instinctively back up when others invade their space. The Chinese reaction is to instinctively step closer.

Despite closer personal space, the Chinese, especially those who are older and in positions of authority, do not like to be touched, particularly by strangers. Do not hug, back slap, or even put an arm around someone's shoulder.

In China, laughter does not necessarily mean that a person is happy or amused. More often than not, a frozen smile or laughter is a defense mechanism used to relieve tension and indicates embarrassment and uncertainty about how to react.

For example, if someone trips and falls over, Chinese bystanders may laugh rather than appear sympathetic, or if someone makes a serious breach of protocol causing embarrassment to everyone, a common reaction is laughter. In such cases, laughter is a tension–releasing device, but it does not imply callousness. Should you find yourself on the receiving end of what seems to be inappropriate laughter, do not get angry. It probably does not reflect amusement at your expense. If you lose your temper, you will likely make things worse and others will probably join in the laughter out of acute embarrassment.

The following table lists some other differences between Eastern and Western gestures.

Body Language	Meaning in North America	Meaning in China
Stamping one's foot	Impatience	Anger, irritation, frustration, remorse
Speaker or performer clapping at the same time audience applauds	Applauding one-self; improper, immodest	Thank you; mutual positive feelings
Staring, gaping	Considered impolite; makes people embarrassed, self-conscious	Curiosity, sometimes surprise
Shushing	Calling for silence	Disapproval, hissing

Body Language	Meaning in North America	Meaning in China
Pat on head	Giving comfort, consolation or encouragement; also shows affection	Seldom used; occasionally adults may pat head of children to show affection; patting the head of a teenager or adult would be insulting
Hand extended toward person, open palm, palm down, with all fingers crooked in a beckoning motion	None	"Come here," beckoning someone to come near
Hand extended toward person, closed hand, palm up, with forefinger only moving back and forth	"Come here," beckoning someone to come near	This same gesture would be considered offensive by many
Forefinger of one hand extended, taps one's own face several times quickly	None	"Shame on you!" playful teasing, semi-serious
Touching or pointing to tip of one's own nose with raised forefinger	None	"It's me," "I'm the one"; to Westerners, the gesture would seem comical

Body Language	Meaning in North America	Meaning in China
Finger snapping	Attract attention, hurry up	Insulting
Using an open hand to cover one's mouth while speaking (generally used by older people)	None	To show confidentiality and secrecy; sometimes no meaning
Using both hands in offering something to a visitor or another person	None	Respect

Conclusion

In the days of affluence, always think of poverty;
do not let want come upon you and make you
remember with regret the time of plenty.

Chinese Proverb

There is an old story, once told to schoolchildren, whose moral was part of the Chinese zeitgeist for millennia.

It is the story of a rich merchant who, through many years of hard work and frugal living, had amassed a small fortune for his family. After a long life he finally lay on his deathbed with his large and prosperous family gathered around to hear his last instructions. Too weak to speak, the old man raised his hand and held up two fingers.

What could it mean? The family was perplexed as to the gesture's meaning until someone noticed they were burning two candles in the room. He went and extinguished one candle and returned to the bedside whereupon the old merchant smiled and nodded his head.

The moral of the story? Burning two candles was an extravagance when one candle was enough.

This is the old China, the China of peasants and villagers and old factory workers. Feast-and-famine is an underlying theme of all Chinese history. Stories of starving villagers exchanging children so they would not have to eat their own are remembered in haunted dreams.

This image of "Old China" exists in stark contrast to the China of today: glass-walled skyscrapers, expensive cars, luxury condominiums, and the ubiquitous Rolex watches and Dupont lighters. In the big eastern cities of Beijing, Shanghai, Shenzhen, and Hong Kong, business moguls, high-ranking bureaucrats, and young executives flaunt their newfound riches in opulent hotels and posh nightclubs.

Between these two extremes lie a thousand shades of gray.

The clash between old and new was never so evident nor discordant as the scene I encountered at a remote Chinese fishing village. Here China had stood still for a thousand years, and the dozen small Chinese houses, with their steep curved roofs and red clay shingles, could have come from a Tang-dynasty watercolor. Being possibly the only Westerner to have visited this remote village, I was not too surprised to see a group of people excitedly running toward me. Naturally I assumed I was the object of this attention because of my uniqueness, but my interpreter, whose English was only slighter better than my Mandarin, explained that they required my immediate help. I was hurried through the cobblestone street and into one of the homes, stepping over the foot-tall doorjamb onto the compacted dirt floor. The interior was from a Pearl S. Buck novel: a coal cooking stove, exposed ceiling beams, red paper lanterns, an altar to the goddess of fishermen, Guan Yin, and the smell of sandalwood incense and fish.

I was still not comprehending the urgent need for my assistance when the group hustled me into another room where, standing on red bricks to raise it above the damp dirt floor, was the largest television I had ever seen. Black and silent like the monolith from *2001: A Space Odyssey,* this alien technology was accompanied by alien instructions—Japanese.

Being a Westerner, I was, they assumed an expert on all things Western, and although the television was manufactured in Japan, it was nevertheless the embodiment of Western technology and thus it was my job to make it work.

I first thoroughly checked to see if there was an "On" switch or some hidden control panel on the TV itself, to no avail, but I managed to confirm that the TV was plugged into an AC outlet and, to my amazement, a satellite cable had been installed. I was then handed a remote that looked like the control panel for the space shuttle. Yet none of the buttons I pushed on the remote would activate the beast. I must have stood there pushing buttons for an uncomfortable 30 minutes with a dozen people anxiously watching my every move. Defeated, I asked as a way of possibly deferring blame onto something else, if there were any other components that came with the TV. Oh yes, but they could not figure out where they fit so they left them in the box. They handed me the box and inside I found three AAA batteries.

And thus I saved the day and can use this story as a twisted metaphor for doing business in China:

Surrounded by 4,000 years of history and tradition, you will encounter leading-edge technology and radical architecture. While haggling over the cost of a dime store knickknack you will be offered shots from a five-hundred-dollar bottle of brandy. While being the center of attention, much of your time will be spent nervously pushing buttons to see what works.

Knowing a little about Chinese business etiquette and culture is like knowing where the batteries go. Then, with patience, trial and error, and a bit of luck, you too will save the day.

Endnotes

[1] Han is the designation for ethnic Chinese. The Mongols and later the Manchu were considered separate ethnic groups.

[2] Jack Beeching, *The Chinese Opium Wars*, Harcourt Brace Jovanovich (1975).

[3] The Country Commercial Guide for China, Bureau of Economics and Business, U.S. Department of State, for Fiscal Year 2001.

[4] U.S. Department of Commerce, International Trade Administration (December 2005): "There are several factors that undermine enforcement measures, including China's reliance on administrative instead of criminal measures to combat IPR infringements, corruption and local protectionism, limited resources and training available to enforcement officials, and lack of public education regarding the economic and social impact of counterfeiting and piracy."

[5] Edward Tse, "China's Five Surprises," *Strategy + Business Magazine* (January 16, 2006).

[6] As told to the author by Greg Jones, at the time an editor and expat living in Beijing.

[7] Hofstede, Geert, *Culture's Consequences: Comparing Values, Behaviors, Institutions, and Organizations Across Nations*, 2nd ed., Sage Publications (2003).

[8] As told to the author by Chris Robyn, an editor and China specialist based in San Francisco.

[9] Marcus Gee, "Green Hats and Other Ways to Blow a Deal in China," *Globe and Mail* (August 26, 2007).

[10] Starting in the '50s when China first opened its doors to foreign diplomats, Friendship Stores were government-run department stores that sold exclusively to foreign diplomats and high-ranking party members. These stores sold consumer items that were not generally available to the public and required a special currency, "Foreign Exchange Currencies" (FEC), that only foreigners could possess (FEC was discontinued in 1994). Today these stores have been all but phased out and replaced by department stores. The Beijing and Shanghai Friendship Stores are the largest of the few remaining in operation.

Bibliography

Brown, Kerry. *Contemporary China*. Palgrave Macmillan (March 2013).

Burger, Richard. *Behind the Red Door: Sex in China*. Earnshaw Books (September 2012).

Callick, Rowan. *The Party Forever: Inside China's Modern Communist Elite*. Palgrave Macmillan Trade (December 2014).

Chan, Savio, and Michael Zakkour. *China's Super Consumers: What 1 Billion Customers Want and How to Sell It to Them*. John Wiley and Sons (September 2014).

Chao, Stanley. *Selling to China: A Guide to Doing Business in China for Small- and Medium-Sized Companies*. iUniverse (November 2012).

De Mente, Boyé Lafayette. *The Chinese Way in Business: Secrets of Successful Business Dealings in China*. Tuttle Publishing (April 2013).

Gallo, Frank T. *Business Leadership in China: How to Blend*

Best Western Practices with Chinese Wisdom. Revised edition. John Wiley and Sons (March 2011).

Hua, Yu. *China in Ten Words*. Vintage Press (August 2012).

Lim, Louisa. *The People's Republic of Amnesia: Tiananmen Revisited*. Oxford University (June 2014).

Lin Justin Yifu, *Demystifying the Chinese Economy*. Cambridge University Press (December 2011).

McGregor, Richard. *The Party: The Secret World of China's Communist Rulers*. Harper Perennial (July 2012).

Michaelson, Gerald A., and Steven Michaelson. *Sun Tzu—The Art of War for Managers: 50 Strategic Rules Updated for Today's Business*. Adams Media (May 2010).

Midler, Paul. *Poorly Made in China: An Insider's Account of the China Production Game*. Revised and updated edition. John Wiley and Sons (January 2011).

Morris, Peter Thomas. *Cantonese Love Songs: An English Translation of Jiu Ji-Yung's Cantonese Songs of the Early 19th Century*. Hong Kong University (1992).

Shambaugh, David. *China Goes Global: The Partial Power*. Oxford University Press (August 2014).

Story, Jonathan. *China Uncovered: What You Need to Know to Do Business in China*. Financial Times Press (April 2010).

Wasserstrom, Jeffrey N. *China in the 21st Century: What Everyone Needs to Know*. Oxford University Press (June 2013).

References

Davis, John Francis, trans. *Chinese Proverbs.* John Murray (1822). Edited by Robert A. Harris (2004).

Nisbett, Richard. *The Geography of Thought: How Asians and Westerners Think Differently . . . and Why.* Free Press (2003).

Sawyer, Ralph D., trans. *The Seven Military Classics of Ancient China.* Westview Press (1993).

———. *The Complete Art of War: Sun Tzu, Sun Pin.* Westview Press (1996).

Sun Tzu. *The Art of War.* Translated by Roger T. Ames. Ballantine Books (1993).

Yang Liyi. *100 Chinese Idioms and Their Stories.* Beijing Commercial Press (1991).

Articles

Barboza, David. "In Cooling China, Loan Sharks Come Knocking." *New York Times International* (October 2011).

BBC News China. "US Report Warns On China IP Theft" (May 2013).

Burkitt, Laurie. "Where Chinese Consumers Are Spending Their Cash." *Wall Street Journal* (March 2013).

Li, Hao. "Doing Business In China: Cultural Differences To Watch For." *International Business Times* (February 2012).

National Bureau of Asian Research, The. "The IP Com-

mission Report, The Report of the Commission on the Theft of American Intellectual Property" (May 2013).

Perkowski, Jack. "Protecting Intellectual Property Rights in China." *Forbes Magazine* (April 2012).

Wang, Shanshan, and Eric Pfanner. "China's One-Day Shopping Spree Sets Record in Online Sales." *New York Times* (November 11, 2014).

Index